W9-CHM-233

In a Blaze of Glory

In a Blaze of Glory

Womanist Spirituality as Social Witness

Emilie M. Townes

ABINGDON PRESS
Nashville

IN A BLAZE OF GLORY
WOMANIST SPIRITUALITY AS SOCIAL WITNESS

Copyright © 1995 by Abingdon Press

All rights reserved.
No part of this work may be reproduced or transmitted in any form or by any means, electronic or mechanical, including photocopying and recording, or by any information storage or retrieval system, except as may be expressly permitted by the 1976 Copyright Act or in writing from the publisher. Requests for permission should be addressed in writing to Abingdon Press, P.O. Box 801, 201 Eighth Avenue South, Nashville, TN 37202.

This book is printed on recycled, acid-free paper.

Library of Congress Cataloging-in-Publication Data

Townes, Emilie Maureen, 1955-
    In a blaze of glory : womanist spirituality as social witness / Emilie M. Townes.
        p.   cm.
    Includes bibliographical references.
    ISBN 0-687-18757-5 (pbk : alk. paper)
        1. Afro-American women—Religious life.   2. Spirituality—United States—History.
3. Womanist theology.   4. Church and social problems—United States—History.   5. United
States—Church history.
    I. Title
BR563.N4T68   1995
277.3'08'082—dc20   94-40244
                                                                                          CIP

Scripture quotations are from the Revised Standard Version of the Bible, copyright 1946, 1952, 1971 by the Division of Christian Education of the National Council of Churches of Christ in the USA. Used by permission.

Epigraph on page 18 reprinted from Cornel West, *Race Matters*. Copyright © 1993 by Beacon Press. Used by permission of Beacon Press.

Quotations of Toni Morrison's *Beloved* are reprinted by permission of International Creative Management, Inc. Copyright © 1987 by Toni Morrison.

95 96 97 98 99 00 01 02 03 04 — 10 9 8 7 6 5 4 3 2 1

MANUFACTURED IN THE UNITED STATES OF AMERICA

For mom and trish

C O N T E N T S

INTRODUCTION
AND
ACKNOWLEDGMENTS

In 1982, the African American writer Alice Walker gave us the definitive understanding of *womanist*.[1] Her four-part definition begins with the origins of the term, the Black folk expression "womanish" or more accurately the expression, "You're acting womanish." Most young Black girls in my part of the South who were precocious, inquisitive, stubborn, ornery—or any combination thereof—were accused of being womanish. It became a mother's (and sometimes a father's) or grandmother's (or sometimes a grandfather's) or aunt's (sometimes an uncle's) or neighbor lady's (and sometimes a neighbor man's) warning about the dangers of Black girls moving beyond prescribed cultural boundaries and socioeconomic determinants. A womanish young Black girl must not only be in charge, a gatherer of knowledge, but she must also be serious about her task. Who she is makes her dangerous to hegemony.

Walker's next understanding of *womanist* is communal. The womanist cares about her people—contemporary and historical. Here Walker challenges us on the nature of how Black folk are with one another. We are sexual beings who are to be loved, sexually or not. We are oppressed people who have had saviors in our midst—sometimes women. We cannot divorce ourselves from one another without killing ourselves and signing the death warrant for our future generations. We must, the womanist must, recognize her location *and* responsibility in a community.

As Walker addresses the origin and the communal dimensions of womanist witness, she turns next to the individual. The individual (as are the other aspects of womanist) is grounded in love. Love of self, love of

9

community, love of the worlds of Black women, love of the Spirit. These are all held together for the womanist—regardless. Spirit, community, and person are held together in a wondrous, if not faithful, circle pointing toward wholeness and hope. Like the flowers in Walker's mother's garden, there is a respect for the possibilities and a staunch will to grasp them.[2]

Her final word of instruction is brief: "Womanist is to feminist as purple is to lavender."[3] This signals the move so many Black feminists have made away from feminist preoccupation with gender inequalities without adequate attention and analytical and reflective insight into the interstructured nature of race, gender, and class oppression—and other forms of oppression as well. The womanist project is to take a fuller measure of the nature of injustice and inequalities of human existence from the perspective of women—Black women.

Womanist reflection is individual, communal, and pithy in its critique and acceptance of love and analysis. Womanist wisdom springs out of the experience of African American women as they have been daughters, wives, partners, aunts, grandmothers, mothers, other mothers, comrades, worshipers, protesters, wisdom bearers, murderers, and saints in African American culture and society—and in the life of the church. This perspective—which flows from surviving, as women, in a society based on inequalities rather than justice—is one that yearns for glory. Such glory is found in seeking a new heaven and a new earth—a world crafted on justice *and* love that holds us all in God's creation rather than in a hierarchy of oppressions.

Womanist spirituality grows out of these roots. This spirituality *is* a social witness. It is born out of a people's struggle and determination to continue to find ways to answer the question, Do you want to be healed? with the Yes! of our lives and the work we do for justice. This book is a way to enter this world, which shimmers with possibilities in spite of the bleak realities of how we are with one another.

I find these possibilities in the collage of Sunday mornings within me. At times they are in my grandmother's church. At times they are in my father's church. It is a collage rich with the tones of worship, the tones of prophecy, the tones of judgment, the tones of getting right with God and Jesus, the tones of Black folk coming together, surviving the blight, gaining spiritual nurture, and being challenged to live their faith and not just talk about it. The Sunday mornings of my life fill the head and the heart. It is in the head and heart where spirituality as social witness is born.

Womanist spirituality is not grounded in the notion that spirituality is a force, a practice separate from who we are moment by moment. It is the deep kneading of humanity and divinity into one breath, one hope, one vision. Womanist spirituality is not only a way of living, it is a style of witness that seeks to cross the yawning chasm of hatreds and prejudices and oppressions into a deeper and richer love of God as we experience Jesus in our lives. This love extends to self and to others. It holds together the individual and the community in a soulful relationship that cannot dwell more on one than the other partner of the relation but holds both in the same frame.

Womanist spirituality is the working out of what it means for each of us to seek compassion, justice, worship, and devotion in our witness. This understanding of spirituality seeks to grow into wholeness of spirit and body, mind and heart—into holiness in God. Such cogent holiness cannot hold its peace in a world so desperately separate from the new earth.

The spirituality that issues from Black women's lives is found in the moral wisdom of African American women. This wisdom can be found in autobiographies, speeches, novels, poems, sermons, testimonies, songs, and oral histories—in their lives. In my attempt to put to paper a spirituality that is lived, I sorted through these possibilities for an entry point. In utter frustration, I turned to my own poetic voice to break the silence. Poetry came as a response to a sermon found in Toni Morrison's novel *Beloved*. The way had revealed itself! As I searched through other novels and consulted with friends, a methodology emerged that seemed true to the experience of Black women's spirituality and moved into a womanist mode of seeking to push beyond what is the ordinary or the norm in Black life, to explore the possibilities.

Thus the constructive chapters 3 through 6 begin with my prayer-poem rooted in the themes of the chapter. This prayer-poem serves as a meditational guide for the chapters as they move from an analysis of novels (chapters 3 through 5) to a consideration of the socioethical issues that the novel presents for the African American community. This is not an exhaustive analysis, but is pointed at key themes I find pressing in Black life and in the life of the African American church. Finally, I explore the ways spirituality as social witness intersects with these social issues.

By contrast, chapters 1 and 2 are descriptive and foundational. Chapter 1 is a historic look at the rise of African American spirituality in its broadest sense. This chapter begins with a focus on the ties that U.S. Black spirituality has to West African spirituality. This blend of African cosmology and Western Christianity birthed a spirituality similar to, but distinct from, the spirituality of the White Western spirituality of masters and mistresses. The effects of the early slave conversions to Christianity in the late 1700s and early 1800s follow. The chapter concludes with a focus on slave spirituals, conversion and salvation, and a look at the moral sphere of Black evangelicalism as it evolved in slavery and into freedom for African Americans.

Chapter 2 focuses on the impact of evangelicalism on nineteenth-century Black women. The resultant spirituality arose in the contexts of domesticity, the cult of true womanhood, and Black evangelicalism. The rise of a strong social reform movement that sprang from Black women's religious worlds concludes this chapter.

Chapters 3 through 6 explore the spirituality and moral wisdom found in three novels by Black women. In chapter 3, *Beloved* by Toni Morrison is central. The sermon the character Baby Suggs preaches in the Clearing to the ex-slaves—children, men, and women—speaks of the nature of being and survival. This raises questions about the reformulation of the nature of ontology and how this becomes a means to understand the nature of lynching—actual and symbolic—in African American life. The historic description of lynching begins the discussion. From there, I look at two forms of contemporary lynching—one imposed on the African American community, one self-imposed by the Black community. The first is environmental racism; the latter is Black neo conservative thought. The quest becomes one of defining the social witness from such radical reformulations of lynching in the United States.

Chapter 4 focuses on the dialogue on the nature of God between Celie and Shug in Alice Walker's novel *The Color Purple*. In this dialogue, the nature of creation and the social witness that flows from it are the heart of the chapter. This leads to a discussion of gender roles in the African American community. I discuss this in the context of cultural images and the ways in which Black society, and society as a whole, shape and are shaped by the power of cultural images.

Chapter 5 explores the sermon of Reverend Morrissey in Paule Marshall's novel *Praisesong for the Widow*. This crucifixion sermon is powerful testimony of death and grace. This chapter focuses on identity and the impact of the color caste (colorism) system within the African American community. Issues of self-worth, self-esteem, and images of blackness frame the discussion in this chapter.

The sixth and final chapter weaves together the themes of the previous three chapters to explore the nature of the apocalyptic in contemporary African American life. The language used to convey this is the image "blaze of glory." This language is rooted in eschatological images of redemption and salvation and is well known and used in Black spirituality. To use the language of glory is to seek a fuller social witness that involves the skills of social analysis, theological and biblical reflection, ethical examination, and mother wit as we examine classism, poverty, and the underclass in the Black community. This chapter is concerned with synthesizing body and soul to provide a vital and faithful alternative to the corporate and individual forms of oppression people face in the twenty-first century.

Womanist spirituality is embodied, personal, communal. I attempt to bring together the historic force of African American women's spirituality with the demand of the Spirit to contextualize and live one's faith. This book is not so much a conversation or a debate as it is my reflections on where and what my life in the Black Church in the U.S. has taught me about faith—my faith. Unlike the modernist search for universal truths, I reflect from the particularity of my own faith journey. Thus, if there are universal truths here, they are unintentional. I seek to speak consciously from the particularity of Asbury United Methodist Church, Mt. Zion African Methodist Episcopal Zion Church, Second Baptist Church, and what I have learned and am learning from the people of faith who have graced me with their lives of witness. It is the particularity of my grandmother, my father, my mother, my aunts, and my uncles. It is the particularity of Cousin Willie Mae, Mrs. Wynne, Mr. Butler, Miss Rosie, and Mrs. Montez. It is the particularity of the Black Church and the women and men who craft it. This particularity, this conscious touchstone, may well manifest dimensions of universality, but it does not exhaust it.

There are many who have helped shape my life and affected my thinking in this book. My family is my benediction from which I come and to which I return. The students, faculty, staff, and administration of Saint Paul School of Theology are a wellspring in my life. I thank the faculty steering committee, Dean Judith Orr, President Lovett Weems, Jr., and the board of trustees of Saint Paul for granting me sabbatical time and resources.

A Younger Scholars grant from the Association of Theological Schools greatly facilitated the writing of this book. As part of the program, Judith Plaskow served as my mentor. It was in an early conversation with her that I confessed my frustration in trying to find a way to put into linear and literate discourse that which is largely oral and nonlinear. Judith suggested that I use my poetry to try to uncover the way to be true both to womanist spirituality and the demands of intellectual rigor. Her suggestion proved invaluable.

The members of Second Baptist Church seek to live the vision of wholeness. We may not always get it quite right as a community of believers, but we do seek faithfulness. To the Reverend Dr. David O. Shipley, the pastoral staff, and the members I will always owe a great debt of gratitude that you welcome me into this church home.

My summer as the Protestant resource theologian in the Tenth Coolidge Colloquium sponsored by the Association for Religion and the Intellectual Life (ARIL) was priceless. Larry Edwards as codirector and Jewish resource theologian, Suzanne Stewart as codirector, John Downey as Roman Catholic resource theologian, and the twenty-four fellows in the Colloquium created a rich dialogue between Jews, Protestants, and Roman Catholics. The time to talk aloud about this project and receive constructive and probing feedback from folks working in a variety of disciplines is something I treasure deep within me.

There are womanist colleagues who continue to be a joy and blessing in my life. The Philadelphia conversation with Katie Cannon and Shawn Copeland added new life to this project. The African American students at Saint Paul School of Theology—past and present—are repositories of hope for me. As I watch and sometimes am privileged to participate in their intellectual and spiritual growth, I am reminded again and again of the goodness of the Lord. Their lives and their vital ministries are testaments to the gift and demands of grace abounding.

Beginning in 1990, I have met with four incredibly gifted and called women over the Memorial Day weekend. Patricia Hunter, Kim Mammedaty, Karla Weber, and Frances Wood live an embodied spirituality that I try to write about in this book. It is our blending of womanist, feminist, and Native American spirits that makes our yearly coming together sacred and holy. The conversation, prayer, song, tears, and laughter invoke the divine among us. It is from our times together that so much of this book began to make sense.

For the memories that are so old, that they are no longer mine.

PART ONE

Moorings

*The black encounter with the absurd
in racist American society
yields a profound need
for human affirmation
and recognition.*

Cornel West, *Race Matters* (1993)

CHAPTER ONE

The Spirit That Moves Us

AFRICAN COSMOGRAPHY IN AFRICAN AMERICAN SYNTHESIS

C. Eric Lincoln suggests that a viable religion is one that has a working reciprocity with the culture that produces it or with which it interacts.[1] Slave religion was a viable religion for the early Africans and African Americans of the United States. Slaves interacted with and adapted to a new land and a new religion. Their blending of West African cosmology and Western Christianity produced a distinct religion that met the needs of those who sought the presence of the divine in the midst of their struggle to survive.

From 1619, when Africans first arrived on United States shores at Jamestown, to 1701, when the Society for the Propagation of the Gospel in the Foreign Parts began to Christianize slaves, Africans in the United States had little to no contact with Christianity. Slave conversions to Christianity did not begin in any significant or recorded numbers until the 1740s during the First Great Awakening.

However, slaves in the South and free Blacks in the North were not without a religious life. With the constant influx of Black Africans through the slave trade, the traditions and religions of Africa were constantly renewed and revitalized in the Americas. Slaves were able to maintain links with their African religious heritage through myths and traditions. Slaves, like those in Liberty County, South Carolina, kept the ways of African spirituality alive by drumming at funerals and dances, with their wood carvings, and the reed baskets and mats they produced.[2] The religious world of the slave was not that of the White master. The former slave Simon Brown's description of how Black people worshiped in slavery[3] demonstrates vividly that the African past exerts a strong influence at the very foundation of Negro religion.[4] Like that of other slaves, Simon Brown's universe was crafted from a blend of West African religions with Christianity. Brown's subconscious was in touch with a cosmology that extended beyond what he saw as the symbols of White religion: pious worship, confinement to church structures, and slavocracy.

Slave Christianity was not cold and proper like its White counterpart. Brown notes that slaves did not have a church structure like Whites, but met in a cabin in cold weather or outdoors under a tree or a brush arbor in the summer. This was not an isolated worship style of Brown's geographic locale. Brown's description is representative of slave worship throughout the South. Fredrika Bremer, a Swedish researcher, offers a description of a Georgia camp meeting that illustrates this. She describes two significantly different religious scenes between African Americans and Whites. In the Black camp meeting "men roared and bawled out; women squealed about like pigs about to be killed; many, having fallen into convulsions, leaped and struck about them so that many had to be held down. Here and there it looked like a regular fight." Bremer described a "quieter scene among the Whites."[5]

Religious dancing and shouting were prohibited by White missionaries, but the slaves danced and shouted in their religious life beyond the watchful eye of White religious authorities. The ring shout, also called "running sperichils," with its circular motion, shuffling steps, stamping, gesturing, and exhorting was kept alive. Bishop Daniel A. Payne of the African Methodist Episcopal Church wrote as late as 1878:

After the sermon they formed a ring, and with coats off sung, clapped their hands and stamped their feet in a most ridiculous and heathenish way. . . . [A slave explained,] "Sinners won't get converted unless there is a ring." Said I: "You might sing until you fell down dead, and you would fail to convert a single sinner, because nothing but the Spirit of God and the word of God can convert sinners." He replied: "the Spirit of God works upon people in different ways. At camp-meeting there must be a ring here, a ring there, a ring over yonder, or sinners will not get converted." [6]

When Brown talks of the slave worship style without a White presence, he notes that "the Spirit would move in the meeting" that "there was a living faith in a just God who would one day answer the cries of His poor Black children and deliver them from their enemies." Brown ends the passage, "But the slaves never said a word to their White folks about this kind of faith." Slaveholders perceived the power and threat of slave worship, and Brown's notation that pater-rollers (White men who terrorized and controlled the slaves) were on hand when slaves gathered for religious purposes supports this.[7]

Slaves conformed to White standards when Whites were present, but when they were left alone, their worship was imbued with the West African notion of the forces of the universe, both evil and good, being at hand and available for consultation and for protection. Also present was the Christian God who would send a man to set the slaves free as Moses had confronted Pharaoh to set the Hebrew slaves free. This was a God who was not wholly transcendent, but immanent as well: "[God was] right there in the midst of them. He wasn't way off up in the sky. He was a-seeing everybody and a-listening to every word and a-promising to let His love come down." [8]

Brown's description of slaves shouting and his description of conversion contain West African religious elements of initiation and possession.[9] When describing shouting, Brown states that "they'd break down and cry like babies or shout until they fell down as if they were dead," which signaled successful conversion. Conversion was contingent upon initiation. The use of the mourner's bench resembles the initiation period described as the training period of seclusion or mourning that new devotees undergo among the Yoruba and other tribes of Dahomey.[10] Seclusion is necessary because it is felt to be dangerous for a person to be possessed without first having proper knowledge of how to cope with the god who enters his or her body.

The evangelical influence is evident in the minister in Brown's description exhorting the sinners to repent and picturing "the poor sinners a-suffering in the fires of everlasting torment." Singing, praying, and clapping to help the mourners to "come through" have definite West African roots. All are forms of religious instruction and acts of contrition or petition.

After the revival meeting, everyone looked forward to the baptism to follow on the next first Sunday of the month. The meeting of the African religious worldview and Christianity occurred vividly in baptism. Melville Herskovits observes that the river spirits are among the most powerful of those inhabiting the supernatural world in West Africa. He describes how "a bedecked procession of worshippers left a shrine atop a high hill, followed a long path to the riverside over two miles away." This is not unlike Simon Brown's description: "Folks would get their passes and come from all around—on foot, in buggies and carts, and on muleback."[11]

The form of baptism practiced is also reminiscent of the art from the tombs of Kongo culture of Bas-Zaire in West Africa. In Kongo culture, the cemetery is a door between the worlds of the living and the dead, which takes its pattern from the circle of the sun around the earth. In the Kongo cosmogram, the cross is an emblem of spiritual continuity and renaissance.[12] The birth of the person is mirrored in the rising of the sun, and his or her death and decline is symbolized by the setting of the sun and its disappearance beneath the sea or earth. In the world below, the dead lose the impurities of life and acquire a new freshness and reenter the world as reincarnated spirits. The sea of the world below in the Kongo cosmogram resembles water in Christian baptism in which all sins are washed away and a "new" person emerges from the water. The power of water found in the Kongo cosmogram clearly was not so quickly forgotten by the slaves as they transformed the Christian meanings of rituals through their understanding of a particular African ritual and religion.

Brown notes that singing is a constant presence in the ritual of baptism. The deacon is dressed in white that echoes the land of things all white of the world below in the Kongo cosmogram. The deacon walks to the appropriate spot in the water with his staff acting as a sounding stick to find the proper depth. This staff is reminiscent of the sign of the elder/chameleon's cane in Kongo cosmology, which is seen as a bridge that puts the living world in communication with the realm of the dead. One could surmise that the deacon was descendant of or representative of those acknowledged as the good leader, the elder/chameleon. The deacon finds and carries the convert to the spot of new life and also returns the convert to shore.

The Christian cross introduced to slaves may have evoked a religious response that was more African in nature than Western. The cross symbolized not only the resurrected Christ, but also a life's journey as the preceding description suggests. The entire symbolic world of Africa did not enter directly into slave worship, but the memory of those symbols was not lost completely. Slaves may not have always been conscious of why certain things were done and how, but they kept those symbols alive through a living faith.

THE EVANGELICAL IMPACT

The evangelical religion of the first half of the nineteenth century provided a refuge for people who relied on their subjective experience rather than on objective knowledge. Evangelical preachers such as Charles Grandison Finney, Lyman Beecher, and Theodore Weld led the Second Great Awakening, which climaxed in 1830–31. This was not a continuation of the First Awakening. The Second Awakening was more secular and more optimistic than the first. It popularized religion while at the same time being larger than merely a manifestation of religion. This new evangelical fervor came at a crucial time in the social life of the country. The United States was emerging from a period of anticlericalism and moving into one of social and cultural disintegration. The traditional connections and boundaries were no longer present for the populace. This left marginalized people searching for new ways to integrate and participate in the growing United States society. Religion and religious communities helped ease the marginality. A key force in religious life was the revivalists. They launched open attacks on the leisure activities (drink and theater) of the new working class because such activities wasted money and blocked the millennium. The pious were clear that they attacked the sin and not the sinner, welcoming all who sought to repent to a home and stability in the social order. As they attacked the leisure activities of the working class, evangelicals poured money into poor congregations and helped establish new churches in working-class neighborhoods. By the mid-1830s hundreds of working-class people in Rochester, New York, like their counterparts in other regions who were swept up in the evangelical impulse became involved in churches. All this activity was understood as an effort to build the kingdom of God.[13]

It is not clear why so many of the working class joined their bosses in this religious revival. Indeed, many workers drew from a tradition of republican skepticism that dated from the Revolution and openly opposed the churches. Free-thought papers printed antievangelical invectives and formal disproofs of the existence of God; they supported strikes and suggested that workers needed education and self-respect more than middle-class temperance sermons.

Hence, the chief social function of religion in the first half of the nineteenth century was its ability to ease the marginality of various groups. It blended the folk beliefs and fetishes that had developed in the African American religious worldview with this evangelical enthusiasm brought to the early nineteenth century by the revivalist movement.

By 1790, the number of slaves raised within a fully developed African culture was only a small percentage of the slave population. More slaves were employing Christian symbols to formulate their conceptions of their origin and destiny.[14] These symbols helped to make sense of their experience of slavocracy and built and kept alive a hope for salvation through freedom. The heavy identification with the Exodus story and the suffering servant Jesus became poignant touchstones for people enduring the yoke of slavery. This suggests that in this emerging Black Christianity social status, race, and illiteracy performed many of the functions of dogma by channeling Black faith. Where dogma functions to provide a framework for good and evil, right and wrong, the social world of the slave with its inherent iniquities *placed* slaves in a context that defined for them that their status as less than human relegated them to their servile positions. Hence, status, race, and education functioned in a deadly triumvirate that provided slaves their religious framework as well. For a people who were inheritors of a worldview that did not separate the sacred from the secular, such social qualities played an enormous role in holding many pious slaves "in their place."

Slave Spirituals

The burst of revivalism helped African Americans and Whites alike to gain reference points in a society that was undergoing drastic change through immigration, the closing of the slave trade, and growing technology. On some levels, Black churches embraced a theology of liberation, self-determination, and African American autonomy. Not surprisingly, an image or understanding of what the second advent of Christ would look like to a people who were enslaved emerged. Yet with Whites keeping a watchful eye on slave religious gatherings, slaves were forced to be careful in their eschatological impetus, so that the untrained or ignorant eye and ear could not catch the this-worldly implications of songs like "Swing Low, Sweet Chariot." While on one level, slaves were singing about their coming glory in heaven, on the other level they were letting one another know when a route to freedom to the North had been found and to prepare to make that journey as well.

Spirituals were drawn from the Bible, Protestant hymns, sermons, and African styles of singing and dancing. The religious music of slaves expressed their faith in powerful and dramatic terms. Albert Raboteau notes the hand-clapping and head-tossing that accompanied the music. Spirituals were not only sung, but shouted and often in the ring shout itself so that the lyrics could be acted out.This was a spirituality of body and soul—a deeply lived and experienced spirituality in which the story of salvation was told both in word, song, and movement.

Conversion and Salvation

Slave and White evangelicalism expressed conversion and salvation differently. Unlike White evangelicalism, which stressed a polarization between individualism and communitarianism and was an "isolating experience of awakening to a deep sense of guilt and sinfulness,"[15] African American evangelicalism was a communal celebration. While Whites felt a need to find signs of redemption in abstinence, bodily inhibition, and withdrawal from the world, African American slaves did not have a need to share these symbols of sinful worldliness, for their world was one of sacred meaning and collective redemption. The ring shout was boldly emblematic of this.

Among African American and White Baptists, salvation was the central theological focus and human repentance and faith were not sufficient to guarantee salvation.[16] The power of the conversion experience was also emphasized by the Congregationalists, the Presbyterians, and the Methodists. The revivals of the nineteenth-century conversion were not a *pro forma* ritual; they were a drama of personal salvation and freedom that demanded moral rectitude from the individual and the community of believers.

White evangelicals experienced conversion as an emotional outpouring of relief for they were now saved from the wrath of God and aware of their imperfect nature.[17] They believed that only a person convicted of sin could receive true salvation. They were prevented from celebrating their salvation because of the guilt and persistent sense of sin. Slaves did not share this sense of original sin. Rather, they prayed to be released from sin in the midst of a physical bondage that could be objectified and cast outside of their souls in a way that was unavailable to their White masters. Donald Mathews notes "the emotional toll of slavery was much more effective than the doctrine of original sin in creating self-contempt."[18] Hence Whites broke down and Blacks were lifted up in their respective experiences of conversion and salvation.

African Americans usually went through a period of personal anxiety concerning their salvation, which lasted from days to weeks. This could take the form of either sitting on the mourner's bench (also called the anxious seat), or being alone in the woods or fields until they were moved by the Spirit. This was an intensely personal, inner-directed phenomenon. The usual sequence of events began with a feeling of sinfulness, then a vision of one's damnation, and finally an experience of acceptance and being reborn by God. The converted man or woman believed that he or she had been with God or that God had been with them. Those slaves who followed the Baptist path could not become members of a congregation of that faith if their souls had not been with God in this fashion.

The White concentration on sin and control of the body as a war between the spirit and the flesh was not shared by slaves. Though both groups experienced conversion by crying out, falling down, and experiencing an ecstatic release, Rhys Isaac posits that slaves and White evangelicals understood these actions differently. For instance, slave religion did not draw a sharp line between the religious and the secular. Therefore, conversion was desired and sought by slaves invested in their salvation. The goal was similar but the worldview and context for conversion between slaves and their White masters and mistresses differed greatly. Indeed by the 1830s, the emotional breakdown of Whites under evangelical preaching became less common and was limited to revivals or camp meetings. The spirituals, conversion, and salvation blended into a bodily felt religious world for the slave. This had moral implications for the slave as well.

The Moral Sphere of Black Evangelicalism

Faced with the yoke of slavery, African Americans could resign themselves to their fate without struggle or they could make a conscious effort at self-determination. Slaves who showed open resistance to White slaveholders actually challenged the theological and sociological dynamics that held slavery in place. Slaves possessed a theological perspective that helped them stand against that of Whites and could provide them with the means to question the authority of slavocracy.

Most slaves, like Simon Brown, were silent on the subject of the hypocrisy of White Christianity. Slaves believed in the ultimate condemnation of slaveholders and any minister who preached a gospel of subjugation. William Humbert, a fugitive slave from Charleston, South Carolina, captures the thoughts of many slaves:

> I have seen a minister hand the sacrament to the deacons to give the slaves, and, before the slaves had time to get home, living a great distance from the church, have seen one of the same deacons, acting as patrol, flog one of the brother members within two hours of his administering the sacrament to him, because he met the slave . . . without a passport, beyond the time allowed him to go home.[19]

From evangelicalism, Blacks inherited a belief system that valued a disciplined person who lived within a disciplined community. African Americans believed that by submitting to such discipline they were in a position to demand that Whites deal with them according to standards that transcended the master-slave relationship.

The experience of Charles Colcock Jones, a White missionary to the slaves, illustrates this point. Jones reveals in his journal his attempts to appeal to the authority of Paul in preaching to slaves against running away. The effect of his admonishments, according to Jones, is that half of his audience walked off and those remaining looked dissatisfied. Jones shares that the remaining slaves expressed their anger and contempt at the close of the service with tremendous vehemence by telling him that there was no such gospel in the Bible or that his sermon was not the gospel. Others took the bold tack of telling him that he was preaching to please the masters and that they would not return to hear any more of his preaching.[20]

Slaves used a variety of methods to reject the slaveholders' gospel. One method was rejection of the master's denomination. Another was a refusal to obey the moral precepts of Whites such as the proscriptions against stealing, lying, and deceit. These were held as virtues by many slaves in their dealings with Whites.[21] Another subtle form of protest was the decision by some slaves to devote themselves to a life of virtue in which they developed a sense of dignity and moral superiority to their masters.

Rebellion was also practiced by pious slaves. Nat Turner, a Black slave who led the best known slave revolt, understood his call to free his people as coming directly from his religious life. His sense of mission and appointed time have clear and unambiguous religious roots. Rebellion, however, was more than sabotage, revolt, or flight. Religion itself was an act of rebellion. Religion and its practice was a way slaves could assert their independence from White dominance and control.

Protest and accommodation were the two poles open to slaves in their religious and secular lives. Evangelical Christianity supported both, at times enabling slaves to choose protest and at other times calling slaves to accept their fate. The protest tradition of the Black Church faded as the century wore on. The militancy represented by African Americans such as David Walker and Henry Highland Garnet diminished as the independent Black evangelical churches began to institutionalize and take on many of the characteristics of their White evangelical counter-parts.[22] Many African American churches in the latter half of the nine-teenth century maintained a policy of silence or apathy on the issue of slavery and equal rights to win public approval and acceptance. Some Black leaders began to reject the establishment of separate Black churches because they believed such churches served to maintain preju-dice and Christian caste.

Yet there are voices that decried silence and apathy, like that of Martin Delany, a supporter of the missionary outreach to Africa, who believed it better to send African American missionaries than White ones to convert the continent. Delany was biting in his criticism of religion in the African American community. He felt that Black churches were imitating the pietism of Protestant evangelicalism and gave African Americans the impression that they were miserable because suffering was a condition to entry into the Kingdom. Delany believed that God helps those who help themselves, and he thought prayer was a foolish means to gain power in the midst of death-dealing structures. He faulted the Black Church's otherworldly stress and saw God as a liberator to African Americans who would claim their future through actions rather than pious platitudes and accommodationist behavior.[23]

The evangelical impact on chaotic social and political order of the United States of the nineteenth century held great promise for the marginalized. A "place" was made for the marginalized and African Americans began to shape a distinctive religious voice that blended African religious traditions and Western Christianity. Raboteau suggests that the revivalistic, inward impetus of evangelical Christianity called forth an egalitarian tendency on the part of Blacks and Whites. This sometimes led to genuine religious mutuality in preaching, praying, and conversion.[24] However the words of Mathews ring a sad note on the promise and the reality:

> The tragedy of southern Evangelicalism was not that its institutions were unable to make white men behave as they should have, but that they could not allow black people full liberty in their Christian profession.[25]

The sense of evangelicalism was to elevate a disciplined self within a disciplined community. Both African Americans and Whites strove to meet this goal with earnestness and passion. However, the catastrophe known as slavery and its companion, racism, prevented African Americans and Whites from carrying the evangelical impulse to its logical conclusion.

Nevertheless, African Americans continued the struggle for full humanity and salvation. African American men and women sought to proclaim their right to freedom by their religious understanding of freedom and a just God. African Americans who responded to the evangelical impulse of the late nineteenth century sought to maintain their dignity and shape a cosmology that affirmed their personhood and self-worth.

CHAPTER TWO

Finding the Legacy

NINETEENTH-CENTURY AFRICAN AMERICAN WOMEN'S SPIRITUALITY AND SOCIAL REFORM

The primary responses of the late nineteenth-century African American woman to her struggle with the narrow space and dark enclosure of racial and economic subordination were expressed through her commitments to religious and social organizations. She espoused a profound spirituality that was forged from the twin hearths of African cosmology and evangelical piety. As we began to note in chapter 1, spirituality was distinct from White evangelical Christianity in form and practice. However both Black and White spirituality provided the framework for women's participation in social and moral reform in the public realm.

African American and White women's religious expression and their spirituality were intensely personal matters. Yet they were able to take their concern for a moral social order that began with their families. They then addressed their concerns to the larger society through associational work and moral reform societies, as well as preaching and exhorting.

The narrow space and dark enclosure Black women endured was one crafted from notions of female subordination. Although subordinate in society, women engaged in moral reform work and participated in the Black women's club movement through an ingenious reappropriation of their role as servant to Jesus Christ. These faithful servants found a rationale and a witness that led them into the public arena to lead reform movements aimed at bringing the kingdom of God on earth. These women held in tension a concern for the individual and the community that was wrapped in a bow of salvation for all of African American society.

FEMALE SUBORDINATION

W. E. B. Du Bois's essay, "The Damnation of Women," in *Darkwater* helps provide the larger context for the subordinate position African American women endured and often challenged in nineteenth-century society. According to Du Bois, Black women existed for Black men and not for themselves in nineteenth-century culture and women sacrificed their intelligence and a chance to do their best work in order to have children.[1] He advocated not only economic independence for women, but also for the right of women to make their own decisions about having children, and did so with an appeal to the effects of constant breeding on the mortality of slave women.

Du Bois presented a fascinating argument that contains elements of the cultic ideal with penetrating social analysis. He was not completely free from the prejudices of domesticity as evidenced when he calls Black women the foundation of the Black Church.[2] He then noted that "perhaps even higher than strength and art loom human sympathy and sacrifice as characteristic of Negro womanhood." Yet Du Bois pointed out that due to the fact that Black women must work to support their families, the family as the ideal of this culture

is not based on the idea of an economically independent working mother. Rather it harks back to the sheltered harem with the mother emerging at first as nurse and homemaker, while the man remains the sole breadwinner. What is the inevitable result of the clash of such ideals and such facts in the colored group? Broken families.[3]

For him, the breakup of families was the result of economics and the modern working conditions and sex roles that hit Black male and female workers. The majority of work available to Black men was below standard while Black women have numerous openings in domestic work and industry.

He decried any attempt to force African American women to return to the home:

We cannot abolish the new economic freedom of women. We cannot imprison women again in a home or require them all on pain of death to be nurses and housekeepers.

What is today the message of these black women to America and to the world? The uplift of women is, next to the color line and peace movement, our greatest modern cause.[4]

His point was to maintain the family unit, but he did not want to do so at the expense of the new economic freedom that he saw Black women enjoyed.

Race, sex, and class are key elements of Du Bois's argument. They are interconnected with domesticity and the ideals of the cult of true womanhood. Du Bois offered a final tribute to the strength of Black womanhood, as he observes:

> No other women on earth could have emerged from the hell of force and temptation which once engulfed and still surrounds black women in America with half the modesty and womanliness that they retain.[5]

Yet Du Bois longed for the day:

> when we will no longer pay men for work they do not do, for the sake of their harem; we will pay women what they earn and insist on their working and earning it; we will allow those persons to vote who know enough to vote, whether they be black or female, white or male and we will ward race suicide, not by further burdening the over-burdened, but by honoring motherhood, even when the sneaking father shirks his duty.[6]

NASCENT WOMANIST THEOLOGY

Although subordinate in status, African American women embraced a witness that challenged their "natural" place in the social order. Black women who were active in the church had a deep, personal relationship with God and Jesus. This was not unlike the experience of Black men who were active in the church. Jesus was not only Lord and Savior, he was brother and friend. Through this personal relationship with Jesus, Black women were able to transcend the inhuman structures that surrounded them in the slave South and repressive North.

At the beginning of the century, religious worship and spirituality were expressed in groups as people gathered to worship in a blending of African survivalisms and White evangelical Christianity. One's spiritual life was shared—conversion, baptism, communion. Increasingly, the joy and release of the ring shout, the spontaneity of spirituals, the appeal to the interrelatedness of humans with nature were lost. African American Christians began a personal journey in their faith.

African American women, however, took an intriguing avenue in expressing their spirituality. Evelyn Brooks Higginbotham notes that Black women in religious circles did not portray themselves as the larger society portrayed White women—fragile and impressionable with little capacity for rational thought.[7] Rather, Black women viewed themselves as having a capacity to influence men and consistently described their power of persuasion over men as historically positive. Such power was not seen as absolute, Black Christians made some exceptions—Delilah and Jezebel were not held up as positive models of female behavior. Black women's biblical hermeneutics reveal women in dual image, just as men were portrayed, and they affirmed their likeness to men and their oneness with men in a joint quest for salvation.

Black women took pride in the mothers of the Bible who became their role models for motherhood. Hence the mothers of Isaac, Moses, Samson, and others gave Black women a view of women as more than bodily receptacles through which great men were born. They saw these mothers as being responsible for rearing sons who would deliver Israel from its oppressors. They drew the obvious parallels for their lives and the lives of Black people in the nineteenth century.

African American women did not break from the orthodoxy of the Black church, but restated that orthodoxy in what Higginbotham characterizes as a "progressive and liberating language for women." [8] Black women took the roles of wife, sister, daughter, and mother, combined them with a personal spiritual experience of God in Christ, and understood themselves to be ministers in their homes. With that step, Black women were able to move on from their image of domestic comforter to a greater call. This was possible through their intense evangelical spiritual drive to live a higher and better life and their concern to shape families and a society that reflected Christian morals and precepts. Black women took the citations of Phoebe, Priscilla, and Mary as coworkers with Paul and translated them into their own work. Their stress was an ultimate allegiance to God, and not to men.[9]

Yet this drive toward Christian moral perfection on the part of Black women did not readily translate into ordination. Perhaps the best example is Jarena Lee (1783–1849). Though she traveled well over 2,000 miles and delivered 178 sermons to spread the gospel, she was never ordained.[10] Lee took the path of soul-saving rather than social reform. She felt salvation forged armor against slavery and racial oppression and prepared Black folk for a future life.

Lee was concerned about social issues, but they were not at the forefront for her. Like so many Black and White women, she experienced an ecstatic religious experience in her call, but fought against the traditional notions of women's image within herself. She did not argue against the high ideals women were held to, but she did argue for a freer interpretation of piety, purity, submission, and domesticity:

> O how careful ought we be, lest through our by-laws of church government and discipline, we bring into disrepute even the word of life. For as unseemly as it may appear now-a-days for a woman to preach, it should be remembered that nothing is impossible with God. And why should it be thought impossible, heterodox, or improper, for a woman to preach? seeing the Saviour died for the woman as well as the man. If a man may preach, because the Saviour died for him, why not the woman? seeing he died for her also. Is he not a whole Saviour, instead of half one? as those who hold it wrong for a woman to preach, would seem to make it appear.[11]

Black women's religious experience in the nineteenth century, after slavery, combined the idealization of the home and motherhood with the attack of the secular woman's movement against sexually exclusive spheres. Higginbotham notes that the dual image of Christ as "feminine and masculine, passive and aggressive, meek and conquering," emerged to inform "their self-perceptions and self-motivations."[12] Higginbotham goes on to note that these women shifted back and forth from feminine to masculine imagery as they described their role in the evangelical crusade of the period. They described themselves both as homemakers and soldiers.

Women were compelled by a deep faith to live out an active witness that reflected the values of their piety. Their associational work became the corporate expression of the individual work they performed in the home in the moral instruction of children and husbands. The urgency of their task was profound. African American women, like White women, could not remain within their homes and see themselves as fully answering God's call to repentance and salvation. Women's associational activities were in direct response to the Great Awakening in which

Protestants tried to counteract the religious indifference, rationalism, and Catholicism of the day to create an enduring and moral social order.

Black and White women developed a spirituality that took them outside of their daily prayer and reflection time and into the world. Their public work was deeply wedded to their inner and intense reflection. The goal was salvation on earth. Because of their unique role in shaping the moral fiber of society through the family, women took up the challenge to spread the promise of salvation. Religion provided a way to order one's life and priorities. It also enabled women to rely on an authority beyond the world of men.

In response to the cultural and religious elevation of the role of motherhood, African American and White women formed maternal societies. Their members gathered to prepare themselves to guide children properly and to raise a generation of Christians. Moral reform societies were begun to eliminate the sin of licentiousness, which appeared in the lust of men and the prostitution of women. They sought to reform and resurrect fallen women and to publicize and ostracize men who visited prostitutes. The focus of moral reform societies was on the family as an arena to solve larger social problems. It was not unusual for the women of these societies to portray females as sacrificial victims to male lust through language that evoked women's power to avenge. Fannie Barrier Williams' words to the board of "Lady Managers" at the World Columbian Exposition of 1893 is a case in point. Williams and other leading Black club women took exception to the exclusion of Black women's contributions to civilization in the exposition. She told the Managers:

I regret the necessity of speaking of the moral question of our women, the morality of our home life has been commented on so disparagingly and meanly that we are placed in the unfortunate position of being defenders of our name. . . . I do not want to disturb the serenity of this conference by suggesting why this protection is needed and the kind of man against whom it is needed.[13]

Later, in 1904, Williams continued her cry:

It is a significant and shameful fact that I am constantly in receipt of letters from the still unprotected women of the South, begging me to find employment for their daughters . . . to save them from going into the homes of the

South as servants as there is nothing to save them from dishonor and degradation.[14]

African American women began with an intense personal experience of the divine in their lives and took that call to salvation into the public realm to reform a corrupt moral order. Their spirituality, which at first viewing resembles a self-centered piety with little relation to the larger context, is an excellent example of the linking of personal and social transformation to effect salvation and thereby bring in the new heaven and new earth. These women sought perfection and advocated social reform in the framework of a spirituality that valued life and took seriously the responsibility to help create and maintain a just and moral social order. These women of the nineteenth century lived their spirituality. They were able to live within the traditional roles handed to them, yet begin to shape and re-form them through their understandings of their ultimate relationship to God. This relationship with God began in the privacy of the home, as "ministers" of their homes and the moral guardians of their families.

AFRICAN AMERICAN WOMEN'S CLUB MOVEMENT AND SOCIAL REFORM

Black club women, like their White sisters, placed a great emphasis on the sanctity of the home and the woman's place in it. There was little direct contradiction of the church's doctrine that females were essentially domestic beings.[15] Like White women active in the club movement, Black women enlarged the concept of domesticity to include areas of interests to club women.[16] They held mothers' meetings involving discussions on "child culture" and "social purity." Their religious beliefs revolved around the dictum that a "woman's true calling is to make people's lives better." This led to an aggressive campaign to convert the "fallen woman" and public denouncement of any man who frequented her company. African American women also verbally accepted the idea that women were the moral guardians of the community.

Both within and outside the club movement, motherhood enjoyed the greatest sanctity. Black women saw Mary, the mother of Jesus, as the personification of the highest expression of womanhood. Although the role of motherhood was dominant, these women also referred to their roles as wives, sisters, and daughters. Male conversion and the ministers' moral rectitude were attributed to "a mother's influence, a sister's guidance, or to the tender persuasion of a devoted wife or daughter."[17]

The effects of domesticity where women's proper role was in the home or domestic sphere were evident in the forming of literary clubs and even night schools for those who worked during the day. The education of the young was the province of women. This responsibility was then extended through the emerging economic and class structure of Blacks to provide instruction to the entire age range of the Black community. Yet all of the educational activities Black women engaged in did not change the prevailing attitudes about the proper role and proper jobs for women. The world of the nineteenth-century woman was one in which the rigid social roles for men and women remained intact. Much of the educational work the women performed through their clubs and night schools did little to challenge the assumed gender roles. The delicate balance between speaking out in the public realm and seeking moral uplift for a whole people was struck with the acceptance, in large measure, of the proper place of women as moral guarantors of the social order.

One striking effect of domesticity on the lives of women was the shift in understanding leisure time and industriousness. With the move toward industrialization and the increasingly narrow notion of women's proper arena as the home, leisure time was an indicator of one's social standing. Middle-class White women, and a much smaller number of Black middle-class women, who were once contributors to the economy of their families, now became models of consumption. White men found the cult of womanhood with its values of piety, submissiveness, purity, and domesticity convenient in an increasingly industrial economy where more men were now forced to leave farming and enter occupations that had been previously held by middle-class White women.[18] When the cult began to dominate with its notion of domesticity, native-born, middle-class White women were replaced by poorer immigrant women as a cheaper, more permanent and exploitable workforce.

Black women were systematically denied easy access to jobs other than domestic work. Women's place was in the home at a time when increasing numbers of poor women and Black women began to enter the wage-labor force. The combined efforts of Black and White women were essential for the progress of Blacks and peaceful race relations. Women believed that Christianizing the home and education were key to solving the race problem. Black women identified with Esther who acted as an intermediary for her race. They saw their role as being similar to hers. Through them, the race would be saved and lifted to greater heights, and African Americans would receive deliverance.

There was also a clear, strong voice within the Black church that carried the mild rhetoric of Black women to its farthest extension. For women like Mrs. G. D. Oldham of Tennessee, women were to be ministers, not slaves to their home.[19] Lucy Wilmot Smith, speaking in 1886 to a predominantly male audience in a church stated, "It is one of the evils of the day that from babyhood girls are taught to look forward to the time when they will be supported by a father, a brother, or somebody else's brother."[20]

The image of woman as loyal and comforting spouse from the cult of true womanhood was transcended to embrace woman's relationship with Jesus. The stress was on an ultimate allegiance to God, not to men. In a strictly biblical appeal, women yoked their faith, with its requirement for support and kindness, with women's domestic image as comforter to support a public responsibility to prophesy and spread the gospel.

Mrs. N. F. Mossell, writing in 1908, gave yet another image of leadership for turn-of-the-century African American women. She believed that the home should be founded on right principles, morality, Christian living, and a "due regard to heredity and environment that promise good for the future."[21] In her truly remarkable work, she deftly handled the social location of women in African American culture while advocating for a wider range of possibilities for male and female interaction and roles:

> Man desires a place of rest from the cares and vexations of life, where peace and love shall abide, where he shall be greeted by the face of one willing to provide for his comfort and convenience—where little ones shall sweeten the struggle for existence and make the future full of bright dreams. Woman desires to carry into effect the hopes that have grown with her growth, and strengthened with her strength from childhood days until maturity; love has made the path of life blend easily with the task that duty has marked out.[22]

In biting advice to newly married women (and perhaps those who had not yet given up on reforming their spouses), Mossell stated:

Keeping a clean house will not keep a man at home; to be sure it will not drive him out, but neither will it keep him in to a very large extent. And you, dear tender-hearted little darlings, that are being taught daily that it will, might as well know the truth now and not be crying your eyes out later.[23]

Further:

The men that usually stay in at night are domestic in their nature, care little for the welfare or approval of the world at large, are not ambitious, are satisfied with being loved, care nothing for being honored . . . . A man who aspires to social pre-eminence, who is ambitious or who acquires the reputation of being a man of judgment and knowledge, useful as a public man, will be often out at night even against his own desires, on legitimate business.[24]

She did not maintain that women should always greet their spouses with a smile, though they should not allow the list of trials Mossell gave to deter them from maintaining themselves in some semblance of dignity and beauty:

Women must not be blamed because they are not equal to the self-sacrifice of always meeting husbands with a smile, not the wife blamed that she does not dress after marriage as she dressed before; child-birth and nursing, the care of the sick through sleepless nightly vigils, the exactions and irritations incident to life whose duties are made up of trifles and interruptions, and whose work of head and heart never ceases, make it an impossibility to put behind them at all times all cares and smile with burdened heart and weary feet and brain.[25]

Mossell's rhetoric is astounding and was even more so given the period in which she wrote. She not only addressed African American society, she also addressed White women of her day:

Hath not the bonds-woman and her scarce emancipated daughter done what they could? Will not our more favored sisters, convinced of our desires and aspirations because of these first few feeble efforts, stretch out the helping hand that we may rise to a nobler, purer womanhood?[26]

Mossell's writings represent in clear terms the ideology of the Black women's club movement. Her concentration on the home, with its foundation being morality and Christian living, represents the combined influence of evangelical Christianity and the cult of true womanhood. Her remarkable ability of providing piercing social commentary while maintaining her role as wife, mother, and supporter of Black social uplift is a key characteristic of the Black women who were active in the club movement. Mossell, like her Black sisters, was trained to strike this balance by Black evangelical Christianity and its demand for a disciplined person and a moral lifestyle. This demand was expanded from a personal spirituality to a concern for the moral fiber of the African American community and United States society. This concern on the part of African American women took its organizational form in the club movement.

Two organizations or clubs had great impact on Black social and political life. The first, the National Federation of African American Women, was composed of 85 groups scattered throughout the country. The larger number of this organization was located in the South. In the August 1, 1895, session held in Charles Street African Methodist Episcopal Church, the organization adopted a twofold agenda:

> (1) concentration of the dormant energies of the women of the Afro-American race into one broad band of sisterhood: for the purpose of establishing needed reforms, and the practical encouragement of all efforts being put forth by various agencies, religious, educational, ethical and otherwise, for the upbuilding, ennobling and advancement of the race;
> (2) to awaken the women of the race to the great need of systematic effort in home-making and the divinely imposed duties of motherhood.[27]

After 1896 and the formation of the National Association of Colored Women, the various women's clubs made no move to standardize their activities. Groups and programs evolved out of the needs of the immediate communities, with common themes being education and care for the aged.[28] Sharecropping housewives, students, salesgirls, dressmakers, artists, teachers, and school principals all came together to form women's clubs for community uplift and support.

One such club was the Washington Colored Woman's League, which was organized 1892. It paid tuition for two nurses in training, contracted to pay one-half of the salary of the instructor for a kindergarten, and established a sewing school.[29] Club women established night schools, worked with prisoners, cared for aged ex-slaves, created insurance-type funds for illness benefits, educated females, and established community facilities.[30] These clubs were the latter-day equivalents of the YMCA, the public library, and the Department of Social Services.

The Belle Phoebe League of the twin cities of Pittsburgh and Allegheny, Pennsylvania provide another vital emphasis for women's clubs. In the League's report to the 1896 convention of the National Association of Colored Women, it gave its object to be:

> Self culture, and to advance the interest of the women of our race on all lines pertaining to the development of a nobler womanhood and the securing of our rights in every legitimate way, and to second the efforts of our leading women such as Mrs. Ida B. Wells-Barnett and others.[31]

Most club members were active church workers or at least attended church. Churches were the major benevolent, spiritual, and social institutions of the African American community.[32] The Black Church opened its doors for the women of the club movement. The 1896 convention of the National Association of Colored Women was held at Nineteenth Street Baptist Church in Washington, D.C. Of the subsequent fifteen national meetings between 1901 to 1930, eight were held in churches.

The second women's organization affecting Black club women on a national level was the National Association of Colored Women. This organization focused on the uplift of the Black peasant woman and the improvement of Negro family life.[33] As Wilson Moses notes, one of its goals was to introduce the standards of Victorian domesticity into the cabins of Georgia and Alabama sharecroppers. There was a decided class bias in the organization with the most influential and dominant members coming from the emerging Black middle class. Josephine St. Pierre Ruffin was a major force in this organization and in the Black woman's club movement in general.

Ruffin founded the Women's Era Club on the belief that the Black women's club movement should be involved in temperance, morality, higher education, and hygienic and domestic questions.[34] The club founded a newspaper, *The Woman's Era*. The paper reflected concerns of the club and, in particular, Ruffin's concerns. It was uncompromising in its defense of Black womanhood and in its condemnation of lynching. The first issue of *The Women's Era* made clear the bias and program of the club:

Up to their [white lynchers] ears in guilt against Negro women, they offer as their excuse for murdering Negro men, Negro women, and Negro children, that white women are not safe from the Negro rapist. . . . We are told that Frances [sic] Willard of America and Laura Ormiston Chant of England, have entered the lists of apologists. . . . Why did not the slaves, when their masters were away trying to shoot the Union to death and keep them forever slaves, out-rage the wives and daughters of these traitors confided in their care.[35]

Black women were no more immune to the nativist sentiments of the period than any other group in the United States. The pages of *The Era* reflected this state of affairs:

The audacity of foreigners who flee their native land and seek refuge here, many of them criminals and traitors, who are here but a day before they join in the hue and cry against the native born citizens of this land is becoming intolerable. . . . self defense and self protection will force this government to protect its own people and to teach foreigners that this land is for Americans black or white and that other men are welcome and come here only by behaving themselves and steering clear of plots and schemes against the people and the citizens who are here by right.[36]

The Black women's club movement came of age when Ida B. Wells-Barnett was attacked by a Mr. Jacks, the editor of a Montgomery City, Missouri, newspaper and the president of the Missouri Press Association.[37] Jacks was both a Sunday school superintendent and the son of a slaveholder. His attack on Wells-Barnett, and then on Black womanhood, was vitriolic and sensationalist. In a letter he sent to Florence Belgarnie of England he claimed:

Out of some 200 [Negroes] in this vicinity it is doubtful if there are a dozen virtuous women or that number who are not daily thieving from the white people. To illustrate how they regard virtue in a woman: one of them, a negro woman, was asked who a certain negro woman who had lately moved into the neighborhood was. She turned up her nose and said, "the negroes will have nothing to do with 'dat nigger,' she won't let any man, except her husband sleep with her, and we don 'sociate with her.' "[38]

Ruffin enclosed this letter in her call to the first conference. However, Moses notes that also enclosed was Ruffin's warning not to give out

Jacks' letter for general circulation or publication. The fear was that the letter was so inflammatory that it would spark violent protest.

Jacks also attacked the character of northern women and British women involved in the antilynching campaign:

> Your pleas seem to us to take the form of asking us to make associates for our families of prostitutes, liars, thieves, and lawbreakers generally, and to especially condone the crime of rape if committed by a negro. Respectable people in this country not only decline to form such associates, but naturally infer that those who ask them to do so and place themselves on a level with such characters must either be of the same moral status themselves, or else wholly ignorant of the condition of affairs here, and consequently do not know what they are talking about.[39]

The reaction to the Jacks' letter was swift and filled with outrage in the various women's clubs. In a letter of one thousand women of Bethel Church in New York, the writers acknowledge that Jacks had spurred a deeply felt need by the various women's clubs to come together and begin to strategize on how to better effect the uplift of the race:

> We are sorry that the "Jacks' letter" should seem to be the prick which stung to activity. We would not have it appear that we are aroused to action only by the irritation of external circumstance, but would be glad for the world to know that, in reality, our women are taking intelligent cognizance of the inner life of the race, and that the desire to be actually noble is more potent than the impulse to resent insult and seek vindication. What we think of ourselves is always more important than what others think of us, that is to say, self-respect based upon truth is the foundation we seek to lay.[40]

The movement focused on both individual and community. It also focused on questions of national import. These women were vitally concerned with racial uplift, but they were also cognizant of the national debates of temperance and morality.

Contemporary womanist spirituality evolves from the nineteenth-century moral reform and Black women's club movements. It is a spirituality rooted in community and concerned for the individual. The piety that emerges is one forged from a history of moral reform and racial uplift work by African American women who sought to live their faith. It is from this witness that I turn to contemporary issues, moral in nature, to tease out the implications of spirituality as social witness.

PART TWO

No Hiding Place Down Here

CHAPTER THREE

To Be Called Beloved

HISTORICAL AND CONTEMPORARY LYNCHING IN AFRICAN AMERICA

to be called beloved
is to be called by God
to be called by the shining moments
be called deep within deep

> *to be called beloved*
> *is more than one plus infinity*
> *more than the million breaths of loving*
> *than the sounds of tomorrow's horizon*

to be called beloved
is the marvelous yes to God's what if
the radical shifting of growth
mundane agency of active faith

> *to be called beloved*
> *is to ask the question*
> *what would it mean*
> *what would it look like if we actually believed*
> *that we are washed in God's grace*

to be called beloved
is to answer the question
we are not dipped
we are not sprinkled
we are not immersed
we are washed in the grace of God

> *to be called beloved*
> *is to listen to the words of Baby Suggs*
> *holy*
> *who offered up to them (us) her great big heart*

"Here," she said, "in this here place, we flesh; flesh that weeps, laughs; flesh that dances on bare feet in grass. Love it. Love it hard. Yonder they do not love your flesh. They despise it. . . . Love your hands! Love them. Raise them up and kiss them. Touch others with them, pat them together, stroke them on your face 'cause they don't love that either. *You* got to love it, *you*! . . . This is flesh I'm talking about here. Flesh that needs to be loved. Feet that need to rest and to dance; backs that need support; shoulders that need arms, strong arms I'm telling you. . . . So love your neck; put a hand on it, grace it, stroke it and hold it up. And all your inside parts that they'd just as soon slop for hogs, you got to love them. The dark, dark liver—love it, love it, and the beat and beating heart, love that too. More than eyes or feet.

"More than lungs that have yet to draw free air. More than your life-holding womb and your life-giving private parts, hear me now, love your heart. For this is the prize." Saying no more, she stood up then and danced with her twisted hip the rest of what her heart had to say while the others opened their mouths and gave her the music. Long held notes until the four-part harmony was perfect enough for their deeply loved flesh.[1]

This admonishment/sermon to love one's heart is an individual and a communal call to question the radical nature of oppression and devaluation of the self and the community in the context of structural evil. This line of questioning can and should take a multitude of directions because it addresses the nature of *systemic* evil, not individual sin alone. My aim is to consider what it means for African American society and culture to love our hearts, to be called beloved, under the rubric of womanist ethical concerns for spirituality, and by praxeological extension, wholeness.

A womanist spirituality is a radical concern for is-ness in the context of African American life. This is-ness is physical and spiritual. Is-ness marks the very nature of our breathing in and out as human beings and the movement of creation itself. This concern for life is not rooted first and foremost in transempirical realities or with a world behind the world of Black life in the United States. Its primary concern is concrete existence (lived life) and the impetus for a coherent and unified relationship between body, soul, and creation. In this sense, it is consonant with African cosmology that understands all of life as sacred. A womanist spirituality seeks to rediscover this apprehension in Black life in the United States.

Because of the nature of its project, a womanist spirituality rejects dualism and argues for wholeness. The subject-other relationship is held in the web of creation or in my terminology, is-ness. This runs counter to the self-other opposition that underlies much of Western thought. This opposition, or split, is a core part of Western values that cannot be ignored. However, while recognizing this split, a womanist spirituality advocates a self-other *relationship,* for it is in the relational matrix that wholeness can be found for African Americans.

This concern for wholeness is shaped within the rise of postmodern discourse as it responds to modernist inadequacies. The irony is that postmodernist discourse often excludes although its theoretical intent is to call attention to and appropriate the experience of difference and otherness as legitimate discourse for critical theory and rigorous ethical reflection. Categories of otherness and difference can swerve toward abstractions at best and become tools for hegemony at worst.

This possibility, which is often reality, is alarming from a womanist ethical stance. The promise of postmodernism is that it provides a way for many to think their way into concrete knowledge of and contact with African American realities. However, when the discourse remains only at the thinking stage, postmodernism commits many death-dealing errors found in modernist assumptions of universal rationality, objectivity, and value-free established knowledge, individuals who create communities rather than being birthed/formed by community, institutionalized radical doubt, and knowledge as hypothesis.

Postmodernism has a radical historicity in which plurality, particularity, locality, context, the social location of thought, and serious questioning of universal knowledge are key features. Such concerns are consonant with a spirituality of wholeness. Issues of diversity and context have long been problematic for African Americans in the United States. Black men and women writers from Phillis Wheatley to Claude McKay to Toni Morrison to Randall Kenan have wrestled with what it means to be Other in our society. They have served as literary critics for how modernist constructs serve to deny, extinguish, and devalue the distinctive features of Blackness and the critical comments of African Americans on life and injustices in the United States.

Black writers have provided a way into the bounty of Black life in the United States. Their work has fed (and has been nourished by) African American intellectuals as well as folks like Miss Nora and Brother Hemphill. The growing body of Black voices in our sociocultural matrix makes it difficult to maintain modernist protestations toward universalities. More than ever before, we are challenged to consider the radical nature of particularity as foundational for ethical reflection.

Although this work has opened greater possibilities for cross-cultural dialogue and understanding, the notion that we are aware of another person's feelings and experiences only on the basis of empathic inferences from our own veers into solipsism. Self-consciousness and awareness of others are not natural dance partners. Understanding the Other is not predicated on how the individual (or the group) makes the shift from the certainty of her inner experiences to the unknowable person. This tenuous shift often produces two outcomes: romanticization and trivialization. African American women and men and children experience racism, sexism, and classism in a multitude of ways. This is borne out in the stereotypical images of Blackness as equivalent to poverty and destitution. Such one-dimensional representations of Black life are narrow, constricting notions of African American life.

Postmodern discourse and analysis that obscures the true diversity of life in the United States for Black Americans collapses African Americans into one grand master narrative. This narrative makes no distinction between the legacy of lynching in the United States, issues and concerns of Blacks in the rural South, or the rise of the Black cultural elite. Black folk become one dark stroke across the landscape of hegemonic discourse. The promise of postmodernism fails its liberative agenda. The call by Baby Suggs to love our hearts is a pithy reminder that particularity is more than an abstract construct of philosophical colloquy. Particularity, historicity, locality, and context all represent human beings. Concrete material existence and abstraction can and should meet in postmodernism. Perhaps Baby Suggs can help us move toward such ontological wholeness in her call to love the "beat and beating heart." One avenue to explore how one loves his or her heart is in her admonition to love a neck unnoosed and straight. This reference to lynching has historical roots and contemporary manifestations.

TO LOVE OUR NECKS UNNOOSED AND STRAIGHT

Lynching a whole people is an obscenity. The specter of the noose is a daily reality for womanist ontological reflection. Baby Suggs again reminds us, "And O my people, out yonder, hear me, they do not love your neck unnoosed and straight."[2] This ever-present reminder of the fragility of life under domination and subjugation is grim reminder that loving the heart is a theo-ethical and political act.

The patterns of southern (as well as northern, midwestern, and western) segregation are our legacy from slavocracy. Racial segregation had its roots in the North where it matured before moving to the South. Although slavery was nearly nonexistent in the North by 1830, a strict color line was in place. Free Blacks enjoyed limited freedom. They could not be bought or sold; they could not be separated from their families; and they were paid for any work performed. The Negro Convention Movement and such figures as Henry Highland Garnet and David Walker illustrate that free Blacks of the North could agitate and organize for racial justice.[3]

However, northern Blacks did not mistake their limited freedom as equivalent to an absence of racism. Whether proslavery or antislavery, the major political parties and their respective constituents believed Blacks to be inferior. Few Whites believed that Blacks had any other place in society than one of subservience. The methods used to assure this place for Blacks in northern society were both legal and extralegal.

By 1860, nearly every phase of Black life in the North was segregated from Whites. Railroad cars, stagecoaches, and steamboats all had special Jim Crow sections designated for Blacks alone. This segregation extended to theaters, lecture halls, hotels, restaurants, and resorts, to the schools, prisons, hospitals, and cemeteries. In White churches, Blacks sat in "Negro pews" or in "nigger heaven" and had to wait to receive communion after the Whites.[4] Until Massachusetts permitted Black jurors in 1855, Blacks could not serve on juries throughout the North.[5]

Northerners contented themselves with a virtually slave-free society. However the presumptions and stereotypes undergirding the attitude of White supremacy and Black inferiority made the North a poor teacher for the South during Reconstruction and beyond.

In the South, the social disorganization of the initial years of Reconstruction (1865–1877) engendered White fear of Black insurrection. Provisional state legislatures adopted the Black Codes designed to relegate Blacks to a presumed inferior place in the southern social, political, and economic structure. The states of Mississippi, Florida, and Texas adopted racial segregation laws for the railroads in their boundaries. The 1866 Texas law was the most extensive requiring all railroad companies "to attach to passenger trains one car for the special accommodation of freedmen."[6] The segregation of the public schools, colleges, jails, and hospitals were all features of Reconstruction and sanctioned by Reconstruction governments.

Simultaneously as segregation became more institutionalized in the South, Blacks began to appear as jurors, judges, legislators, voters, and merchants. *The Standard* of Raleigh, North Carolina noted "the two races now eat together at the same table, sit together in the same room, work together, visit and hold debating societies together."[7] Although the observations of the newspaper were not the norm for the South, there was some movement to mix the races.

The Reconstruction Act of 1867 with its incipient Jim Crowism drew heated protest from some Blacks. Demonstrations in New Orleans, Richmond, Virginia, and Charleston, South Carolina, focused on segregated streetcars. The 1868 state legislatures of South Carolina and Mississippi received demands from free Blacks that the civil laws protect their rights on common carriers and public accommodations.[8]

However, these acts of radical protest were not the norm for the majority of Blacks. Blacks rarely entered public accommodations that were clearly inhospitable. Black leaders drew a distinction between social equality and public equality and sought the latter. In the mind of these leaders, public equality meant civil and political rights.[9] This form of equality recognized the humanity of Black folk. In acknowledging this humanity, Black leaders pushed for civil rights. Social equality was an unthinkable goal, even to activists such as the young W. E. B. Du Bois. Social equality meant a transformation of the natural order.[10]

C. Vann Woodward credits the South's embrace of extreme racism with the relaxation of significant opposition to racism by the liberal North, the decline of the power and influence of the southern conservatives, and a corollary decline of the influence of the idealism of the southern radicals.[11] When the liberal North agreed to the Compromise of 1877, this signaled the beginning of the North's retrenchment on race. Eventually the North and South differed little on their race policies. Northern liberals and abolitionists began to voice their belief in Black innate inferiority, shiftlessness, and hopeless unfitness for full participation in the White man's civilization.[12]

By the beginning of the 1890s the door was wide open for untempered racism in the South. Economic, social, and political encumbrances combined to create a social and economic depression. Social and political reforms did not materialize in the manner hoped for, leading to further frustration. In this climate, the South sought a scapegoat. With the sanctions against racism lifted, Blacks within the United States became the target of White frustrations.[13]

Radical racists believed there was no place for African Americans in the South or in the United States. Joel Williamson observes that the advocates of radical racism believed the end might come in a race war that the superior Whites would win.[14] The bottom line for the adherents of radical segregation and racism was that Whites and Blacks could not live side by side on United States soil.

In 1898, during the northern retreat from the South and the North's increasing disinterest in emancipated Blacks in the South, the United States expanded into the Pacific and the Caribbean. This expansion brought eight million people of color under United States rule and dictate.[15] The attendant attitude of imperialism is found in the pages of *The Nation* magazine that responded matter-of-factly, "of course, [they] could not be allowed to vote."[16] The ideology of racism extended beyond African Americans in the continental United States to include Hispanic, Asian, and Caribbean peoples.

This is the context for lynching as it emerged from an area on the south side of the James River in Virginia to become a national phenomenon in the late eighteenth century.[17] This form of punishment consisted of thirty-nine lashes that were inflicted without trial or law, but on the suspicion of guilt that could not be "regularly proven."[18] By the nineteenth century, especially after the Civil War, murder became associated with lynching. The reasons given for lynching ranged from rape and murder to mistaken identity.

Rumors of rape became a "folk pornography" in the South.[19] Jacquelyn Dowd Hall notes that the fear of lynching served to hold both Blacks and women in their respective places as subordinate to southern White men. She states it is "no accident that the vision of the Negro as threatening beast flourished during the first organizational phase of the women's rights movement in the South."[20] Lynching served as severe sanction against voluntary sexual relations between African American men and White women. In addition, lynching served to reenforce the hierarchical power relationships based on gender.

Southern Whites followed a Victorian model for sex and family roles.[21] Men viewed themselves as providers and protectors and women were the moral guardians of the home. In the Reconstruction and Redemption eras this model evolved such that White women and Black women, like male and female slaves before them, were viewed as the property of white men.[22] White men could not tolerate the image or the reality of Black men crossing the color and caste barrier to have intimate relationships with White women. However, the prevalence of miscegenation before, during, and after slavery shows it was permissible for White men to have such relations with Black women.

Lynching was not an activity carried out by a small group of people avenging the rape of White womanhood. It involved large segments of the populace. Hall notes that it was often the presence of "men of property" leading the lynch mob that caused sheriffs to demur from upholding their legal responsibility to keep the peace.[23] In rural areas, planters sometimes used lynching for coercion and increased profit. The incidence of lynching rose in the summer months after the planting season when all that remained was the profitable harvest season.[24]

Mob violence was the instrument to maintain segregation and solidify a rigid caste division between racial groups that were bound to the same society, legal system, and economy. The drive to maintain White superiority is tied to what Hall attributes to a siege mentality. She writes, "Whites felt themselves continually under siege. Lynching persisted as much to reaffirm solidarity and demonstrate power *to whites themselves* [her emphasis] as to punish and intimidate blacks."[25] Continuing this line of insight, Fredrickson notes that the prime agent of white-supremacist terror in the South was the mob.[26] He posits that the white power structure of the South was "relatively fragile" because it did not have within it systematic control over Black social location, movement, and labor.[27]

In the contemporary era, such control *is* systematic. The nature of structured social inequality in United States society is such that peoples are confined and warehoused either by choice or by condition. The rise of the suburbs represents chosen segregation and control. Rural poverty and urban blight are representatives of conditioned segregation and control. We are living in a system that has no heart, little compassion.

Baby Suggs's words are pithy instructions for womanist ethical reflection:

And no, they ain't in love with your mouth. Yonder out there, they will see it broken and break it again. What you say out of it they will not heed. What you scream from it they do not hear. What you put into it to nourish your body they will snatch away and give you leavins instead. No, they don't love your mouth. You got to love it.[28]

To love the mouth, the eyes, the hands, the neck, the heart—to love the body is radical spirituality within structured domination and control. The concerns for concrete material well-being *and* spiritual wholeness are imperatives in the postmodern context for African Americans.

TO LOVE OUR EYES AND HANDS

Contemporary versions of lynching a whole people are toxic waste landfills in African American communities. Toxic waste facilities are often located in southern communities that have high percentages of the poor, the elderly, the young, and people of color. There is an excessive concentration of uncontrolled toxic waste sites in Black and Hispanic urban communities.[29] Southern Black rural communities are home to large commercial hazardous waste landfills, disposal facilities, and incinerators. These businesses are touted as tools for economic revitalization and necessary for the safe conversion of toxic waste to forms of safe energy and harmless compounds. Often, local governments and the waste industries minimize the impact of the contamination of the soils outside the immediate site areas and the effect this contamination has on surface and subsurface water supplies.

Blacks and economically disadvantaged groups are often concentrated in areas that expose them to high levels of toxic pollution—urban industrial communities and rural areas.[30] In comparison to suburban areas, air pollution in inner-city neighborhoods can be up to five times greater. Racial/ethnic and low-income folk suffer from unregulated industrial growth (or the lack thereof), poor regulation of industrial toxins, and public policy decisions that favor those with political and economic clout. This clout controls land use.

Another feature of toxic waste landfills is sparseness of population. Large toxic landfills are usually not found in major metropolitan areas. Competing uses drive up the cost of urban land and the threat to the public safety of a large population moves large toxic waste sites to the more sparsely populated areas. In the South, the population of poor and sparsely populated rural areas are most likely to be Black. When density of population is a key criteria for siting toxic waste facilities, the effect is to target rural Black communities that have high rates of poverty.

The historic 1984 General Accounting Office (GAO) study of four hazardous waste sites in the South found a strong relationship between the location of the sites and the race and socioeconomic status of the surrounding communities.[31] Three of the four locations had majority Black populations. More than one-fourth of the population in the four communities were below the poverty level. Most of these poor were African Americans. The nation's largest hazardous waste landfill is in predominantly Black and poor Sumter County in Alabama. This landfill receives toxic materials from 45 states and several foreign countries. Counter to the usual placement of hazardous waste facilities in rural areas, the predominantly Black and Hispanic southside of Chicago has the greatest concentration of hazardous waste sites in the United States. In Houston, Texas, six of the eight municipal incinerators and all five municipal landfills are in predominantly Black neighborhoods.[32]

Nationally, there are twenty-seven hazardous waste landfills operating in the continental United States. Large commercial toxic waste landfills and disposal facilities are more likely found in rural communities of the southern blackbelt. Nine landfills (33 percent) are in Alabama, Louisiana, Oklahoma, South Carolina, and Texas. These nine landfills represent almost 60 percent of the nation's total hazardous waste landfill capacity.[33] The four landfills in the areas with majority Black populations account for 63 percent of the South's total hazardous waste capacity. Of the four, three alone account for almost 59 percent of the hazardous waste landfill capacity.

The 94 uncontrolled toxic waste sites in Atlanta bring the devastation to microlevel. Just under 83 percent of Atlanta's Black population live in these waste site areas. This compares with just under 61 percent of the White population living under the same conditions. Both figures are unconscionable, yet when Blacks and Whites are forced to endure toxic waste, African Americans always suffer a greater burden. There is something askew when over 15 million African Americans and over 8 million Hispanics live in communities that have one or more hazardous waste sites. Blacks are overrepresented in metropolitan areas that have the largest number of uncontrolled toxic waste sites.[34]

A comparison between the hazardous waste sites in Baton Rouge, Louisiana's ten largest White and racial/ethnic communities covers 20 toxic waste sites. In these 20 communities, the toxic waste is nearly seven times the national average on a per capita basis. Alarming as this may be, it becomes more so when a closer look reveals the nuances of the sites. The White communities have five sites that account for less than 1 percent of the hazardous waste. The fifteen sites in the racial/ethnic communities house over 99 percent of the hazardous waste.[35]

The reality is that African Americans in the South bear a heavy burden. They not only battle spiraling crime rates, drug trafficking, deteriorating infrastructures, high unemployment, poverty, and the farm crisis; they also receive a great deal of hazardous trash that threatens to rip to shreds any love of heart or notion of belovedness.

African Americans, as a community, are forced to combat structural barriers that confine large segments of Black people in less than desirable physical surroundings, reduced housing and residential options, and limited mobility. Housing and employment discrimination; redlining by banks, mortgage companies, and insurance firms; public policies that give preference to the affluent; and unequal law enforcement of land use and environmental regulations are effective barriers to a communal love of heart.

Federal housing policies sharply defined residential and economic options for many African Americans. Institutional and individual discrimination in housing markets, geographic changes in urban centers, and limited incomes physically trapped millions of urban and rural African Americans in inner cities. Government housing policies fueled the White exodus to the suburbs and accelerated the abandonment of the core of urban cities.[36] White-collar jobs and jobs in the service occupations moved to the suburbs. The federal and state funding of the freeway and interstate highway systems were keys in this exodus. The construction of highways and interstates often cut through racial/ethnic neighborhoods and public transportation often did not (and does not) keep pace with the economic move out of the city.

Communities lose their economic heart and become social prey for ill-advised or ill-conceived income generators such as toxic waste sites and industrial pollution. The results were and are not only economic; they are health related. When the air is bad, communities suffer from higher risks of emphysema, chronic bronchitis, and other chronic pulmonary diseases. This is the fate of the Black community in the urban core.

Paper mills, waste disposal and treatment facilities, chemical plants, and now hazardous waste landfills were businesses that found the South to be the logical place to go in the 1970s. The "new prosperity" of the South was largely a metropolitan phenomenon. Communities that were economically depressed became attractive locations because they represented a source of cheap labor. The good business climate of the South features a large pool of tractable and nonunionized labor. Because of business policies that feature the systematic avoidance of urban ghettos and rural blackbelt communities, jobs are scarce. In some of these communities, leaders believed that having any development was better than no development. The sight and smell of paper mills, toxic waste incinerators, and chemical plants became the trade-offs for having jobs near economically depressed communities. Toxic waste and other environmental problems have become linked to the state of the economy of a given community. The hoped-for economic trade-offs did not materialize. The living conditions in many Black communities have not improved noticeably with the new growth.

The Black community has begun to challenge the legitimacy of environmental extortion as adequate mortgage for the health of the community and that of future generations. Baby Suggs's words to the community of ex-slaves ring true:

> They don't love your eyes; they'd just as soon pick em out. No more do they love the skin on your back. Yonder they flay it. And O my people they do not love your hands. Those they only use, tie, bind, chop off and leave empty.[37]

The early 1980s saw the beginning of the response to love the eyes and hands. This was when the people in the communities began to draw connections between civil rights and environmental problems.[38] This growing awareness was fueled by what residents saw as unfair, inequitable, and discriminatory practices toward the poor and people of color. The key is that in loving the heart, it was the Black community that had to speak out for its survival. Those Black folk who live in the community became (and now become) the advocates for healthy communal survival and the eradication of toxic manna from human progress.

A major obstacle to survival for African Americans in this postmodern age is information. Placement of toxic waste sites often occurred with little community participation and little awareness of what the site would actually house. Sumter County, Alabama, is not unusual in the saga from communal ignorance to awareness. This site is the largest hazardous waste facility in the United States. It was originally a smaller landfill partly owned by the son-in-law of former Governor George Wallace. When Chemical Waste Management, Inc. (owner of four of the six largest landfills in the nation which account for over 50 percent of the permitted hazardous waste landfill capacity in the United States) bought and expanded the site in 1977, there were no laws that dictated public hearings. The residents thought that the plant produced fertilizer. This was a welcome addition to a highly depressed economic area. The truth of the Sumter facility did not emerge until workers began to complain about working conditions and health problems.

The world behind the Sumter facility reveals a devastation of the heart. Sumter County is nearly 70 percent Black. Most of the population of 17,000 is located in the southern half of the county where most of the White population lives. The small town of Emelle is the closest community to the landfill and in the more sparsely populated and predominantly Black northern half of the county. The minority White and majority Black populations live separate social lives—cemeteries, churches, schools. The minority White population dominates the economic arena and controls most of the businesses, farms, and timberland in the area.

Sumter County has experienced significant outmigration that has combined with the decline in the historic base of the economy, agriculture. During most of the 1980s, unemployment fluctuated between 12 and 22 percent.[39] Chemical Waste Management is the county's single largest employer, and it channels $15.9 million into the local economy. This includes a surcharge on each barrel of waste transported to the site that then goes to help support the school system.

The struggle for political power began in the 1960s when Blacks finally won the right to vote. By the early 1970s, the Federation of Southern Cooperatives established its main training facility in Sumter County. This helped to strengthen the local Black political organization and the initial quiet presence of Chemical Waste Management did not go completely unnoticed. In 1981, Black leaders played an important role in alerting the public to the dangers of the Emelle facility. The call to heart was embodied in the community-based and community-led demonstrations at the facility. Black communities may not have a long history of dealing consciously with environmental problems, but groups that do tackle environmental racism in the Black community often arise from the Black Church, civil clubs, neighborhood associations, community improvement groups, antipoverty and antidiscrimination organizations.[40] The yoking of civil and environmental rights is crucial to ontological wholeness.

Loving our heart is not an exercise in individualistic nihilism. It is a radical, and often communal, response to cultural, social, religious, economic, and political hegemony masquerading under the guise of cultural heterogeneity. Disproportionate stationing of toxic waste sites in poor Black southern rural communities is a cruel irony of progress. This progress is marked with the stench of domination and control. The growing protest among southern Blacks against the toxic waste dumped into their lives yokes testament and agency. To love one's heart is to care about one's environment, to strategize and anticipate the future, to draw on the community of resistance and solidarity.

FLESH THAT WEEPS, LAUGHS, DANCES

Toxic waste landfills are imposed on a community. However, there is a form of lynching that comes from within the community. Recent neoconservative and conservative African American theorists can splinter the deep connection between resistance and solidarity. Baby Suggs's reminder that "we flesh; flesh that weeps, laughs; flesh that dances on bare feet in grass" is made into a lesser order of creation. And the ontological demand to "Love it. Love it hard" is lost in a modernist drive to become one in the melting pot of United States culture. African American culture and society are more complex than much Black neoconservative and conservative thought allows.[41]

In 1990, median family income in current dollars for Blacks, Whites, and Hispanics rose significantly from the 1980 figures. However, when adjusted for constant 1990 dollars, the increase is far from dramatic. The figures suggest that everyone (but those who are in the upper and elite income brackets) in U.S. society is surviving progress, but not thriving.[42] Black Americans trailed Whites and Hispanics in median household income as more folk in each racial/ethnic group slipped below the poverty line from 1980 to 1990.[43] When factors such as birth rates, death rates, net immigration rates, education, employment, the shifts that occur when the number of wage earners in a family are factored, health statistics, and so forth, a simple picture of life for African Americans in the United States is impossible.

To love the flesh, to care for people's lives is crucial in times such as these. The very is-ness, the ontological wholeness of African American society and culture is at stake in such a complexity of information. In 1959, 55 percent of African Americans were officially poor. Today that figure is near 36 percent. While we celebrate this shift out of poverty, it cannot be done without realizing that in 1969, 32 percent of African Americans were poor, in 1974 only 30 percent were poor.[44] The poverty rate for Blacks is three times that for Whites, and education does little to diminish the wide poverty gap between Blacks and Whites. Although a high school diploma decreases the chances that Blacks will live in poverty by 50 percent, the same diploma decreases this possibility for Whites by 75 percent.

In the midst of this austere conundrum, sociologist William Julius Wilson tried to explain the evolution of race and class in United States history and the factors behind urban Black economic problems. His 1978 study of this, *The Declining Significance of Race,* suffered from a misleading title that helped attract a firestorm of criticism. Wilson's thesis is that the economy and the government interacted in various historical periods to structure social relations. This produced different contexts for racial antagonism and different means of access to power and privilege. From this sociohistorical approach, Wilson posits that in the late 1970s, economic class was a more important factor than race because more Blacks had made it into the middle class. The highly nuanced nature of Wilson's argument was lost on his detractors.[45]

Wilson responded to this criticism in his 1987 work, *The Truly Disadvantaged.*[46] His aim was to provide the outline for a more informed urban policy. He explored the social class polarization between middle income and lower class Blacks. In doing so, Wilson challenged liberal and conservative assumptions and approaches to issues of poverty and race. Wilson rejected liberal refusal to employ such terms as *underclass,* the emphasis on selective Black achievement and the denial of the existence of social disruption, and the tendency to emphasize racism as the sole explanation for urban problems. He rejected the conservative thesis that economic success stems from cultural characteristics and its estimate that the rise of female-headed households among Blacks is caused by liberal social policy, welfare dependency, and permissive attitudes. For Wilson, the rise of the Black underclass lies in Black male joblessness, the economic disinvestment in the central cities, and other economic factors. He advocates a program of economic reform, a comprehensive democratic agenda to rebuild the central cities, and the creation of new jobs and opportunities. Wilson suggests that racial prejudice will disappear because it is a barrier to an expansive capitalist economy. However, he does believe that affirmative action policies and other race-sensitive measures are necessary as long as the United States has a racially stratified workforce. Wilson's work has forced a reinvigorated discussion about the root causes of poverty.

Part of this discussion was led by many upper middle-class Blacks after the 1984 Ronald Reagan presidential landslide victory. These Blacks became increasingly vocal about the limitations of supporting the Democratic Party and advocated aligning with the conservative majority of Whites who were now the more influential sociopolitical and economic group in the U.S. Further, these new Black conservatives argued that Blacks needed to conform to the new reactionary political realities and become active participants in entrepreneurial capitalism.[47]

Shelby Steele's *The Content of Our Character* is a case in point. Steele argues that the 1954 Civil Rights Bill was passed on the understanding that equal opportunity wouldn't mean racial preference. He believes that affirmative action moved from antidiscrimination enforcement to social engineering. For Steele, the imposition of affirmative action goals and timetables creates a false sense of pluralism and equality inside college campuses because most Blacks are not culturally or intellectually prepared to compete with Whites on an equal basis. What we achieved, according to Steele, was a type of cosmetic diversity that did not address the roots of African American deprivation. All in all, affirmative action has caused Whites to draw the inaccurate conclusion that all Blacks, regardless of their talent, achieve due to their race. Steele tells us that preferential treatment translates into a lowering of standards to increase Black participation. This then spawns debilitating doubt that undermines African American performance in the public realm.

In *Civil Rights: Rhetoric or Reality?*, Thomas Sowell claims that recent immigrants such as Asians and West Indians who became racial minorities in the United States are significantly more successful than native Blacks and rival Whites in achievement.[48] He neglects to address the fact that due to the highly selective U.S. immigration policies for Third World countries, many of these recent immigrants are skilled and educated workers—scientists, engineers, doctors, and academics. Asian immigrants have drawn disproportionately from the occupational elites, but more recent Asian immigrants include a large number of unskilled and uneducated workers. These folk stand in stark contrast to the elites.[49] Black West Indian immigrants have been more successful than African Americans. However, Sowell does not address the racial situation in the West Indies in which there is virtually no White working class and Blacks hold the majority status. Therefore, Blacks in the West Indies have full access to acquiring skills.

Steele and Sowell should have stood in the Clearing with Baby Suggs and the other women, men, and children. The lesson for African Americans in the Clearing is that we have learned to hate ourselves without even realizing the level of our self-contempt. In loving ourselves, developing our hearts, we must become our own best critics and our greatest cheerleaders for justice and hope. Such arguments as Steele's fail to consider the nature of structured social inequality. They represent modernist notions of individualism and an ease with systems that promise diversity, but are structured to deny diversity's concrete demands for change.

The gathering in the Clearing of Baby Suggs and "every black man, woman and child who could make it through"[50] was a communal call to gather into wholeness away from the racist assaults of White folks. This *could* be a reinterpretation, if not a recasting, of Black separatism. The point in their gathering is not to create a separate identity—this was accomplished at their births. The people gathered themselves into a place of political and spiritual sanctuary. In that place, they began to re-member themselves through laughter and tears and dance and song.

Steele's work is part of a historic stream in which structures of domination have relied on Black conservative (and now neoconservative) politicians and intellectuals to justify patterns of race, class, and gender inequality. Manning Marable points to ways in which corporate America has used the ideological and social class diversity within African American society and culture. He notes that the head of Clairol endorsed the 1968 Black Power Conference held in Philadelphia by stating the demand for Black power means "equity, empowerment—ownership of apartments, ownership of homes (and) ownership of businesses" for the Black elite. In 1978, Gulf Oil funneled $50,000 to the Reverend Ralph David Abernathy (then head of the Southern Christian Leadership Conference), $55,000 to the Reverend Leon Sullivan's Opportunities Industrialization Centers, thousands more to other Black cultural groups and civic leaders when Gulf was being boycotted by Black activists for its financial support of the repressive Portuguese colonial government.

Black neoconservatives such as Thomas Sowell, Glenn C. Loury, J. A. Y. Parker, and Clarence Thomas gained notoriety during the Reagan-Bush era. Each took aim at affirmative action out of the belief that affirmative action does not help poor Blacks, only middle-class ones (like themselves). This denatured view of African American life focuses solely on poor Blacks rather than the complexity of the African American socioeconomic structure. The solution becomes naively monochromatic rather than multifarious. Each socioeconomic class within African American society faces particular manifestations of racism, sexism, and classism. The ultimate goal of affirmative action is occupational integration no matter a person's gender, race, or class. Affirmative action is not a panacea for the injustices of structured social inequality, but it is one helpful social instrument to begin to bring all of us back to the embodiedness of Baby Suggs's sermon in the Clearing.

William Julius Wilson grants that some disadvantaged Blacks have benefited from affirmative action, but those of ghetto underclass have not. He gives us a much more complex notion of Blacks in poverty. The underclass is outside the occupational system due to little or no job skills, long-term unemployment, poverty, criminal activity, and welfare dependency. These are folks who are so destroyed as persons that they are unemployable and untrainable.[51] For these people, Wilson suggests, affirmative action will not help. However there are disadvantaged Blacks in the underclass who are motivated for work and training if there is access to employment. For this group, affirmative action is a viable and necessary option.

To stand with Baby Suggs in the Clearing is to listen to the diversity of voices hearing her words of challenge, hope, and comfort. Each heard her call to love eyes, back, hands, mouth, feet, shoulders, arms, neck, womb and private parts, and the dark, dark liver from where they lay in the Clearing. They formed a community in the Clearing, but each came with their own trail of living. This is how we are in our radical is-ness in African American society and culture today. A womanist spirituality based on wholeness recognizes this intricate social network of Black society.

TO DANCE WITH TWISTED HIP

Perhaps postmodernist discourse can provide us with the tools in womanist ethical reflection to continue to explore this bonding between body and spirit. However, the danger lies in abstractions. The notion of the Other is not always a helpful category to tease through the thorny, concrete issues of body and spirit. The Other, linguistically, seems too sterile a category for a people who have been told to love the dark, dark liver. The Other can be a category of avoidance rather than is-ness, a category of abstraction rather than concreteness. The Other can lean heavily toward reductionism and denial of truth, toward indignity and injustice. Like all human constructs, notions of Otherness and particularity and pluralism can become categories that objectify and possess rather than open new ground for genuine dialogue and transformation.

At the heart of a womanist spirituality is the self-other relation grounded in concrete existence and succored in the flawed transcendent powers of our spirituality. The legacy of lynching, the siting of toxic waste dumps, and the rise of influential Black neoconservative thought— each signals the need for a spirituality of wholeness in which the self-other relationship becomes primary. Although these are only three moments in the stream of Black life in the United States, they indicate the kind of rending of body and soul that disseminates African American society and culture.

We make ourselves the oppositional Other, we turn to forms of self-hatred and self-destruction. Instead of critiquing and then working to eradicate notions of individualism, we forget our African past and seek to establish our lives as separate from one another. To recognize the differences in the socioeconomic structure of Black life does not mean that African Americans are free to cut those who are not in our social class or gender adrift from our lives. To divorce civil rights from environmental concerns is to live in a deadly dualism in which there will be no air to breathe. To practice historical amnesia about the legacy of lynching in the United States is to doom all of us to find new material to construct postmodern nooses.

Perhaps these cautions will be enough to hold womanist ethical reflection to a rigorous and articulate witness that avoids reductionism in articulating the experience of living and loving in African American life. Rather than intellectually tempt our work with the luxury of competing narratives, wholeness demands the whole truth—our lives are complex and have layers of experience in each moment.

To remember our fleshiness is to recognize that dualistic oppositions such as self-other, egoism-altruism, theory-practice, individual-community, and mind-body are interactive and interdependent in a spirituality of wholeness. Each is relational and historical as it informs the other. Awareness of this complexity of African American life helps guard against reductionistic claims about who Black folk are and what they do. A people who run the gamut from Phillis Wheatley to Henry Highland Garnet to Alexander Crummell to W. E. B. Du Bois to Septima Clark to Martin Luther King Jr. to Victoria DeLee cannot be easily defined or understood.

Defining Black people's otherness or subjectivity as victimization is a hollow and incomplete description of is-ness. We have narratives of resistance and rebellion as part of our story as well. Yet we must not rush too quickly to celebrate the victory of our diversity. Resistance is not synonymous with self-actualization on an individual or collective level.

A womanist spirituality of wholeness is, finally, radically relational. The various narratives of African American life are constituent of the grand narrative of Black faith and hope in this land. This relational character calls us to moral responsibility and accountability for our lives and the lives of all those who have survived the diaspora. We are, in the most basic sense, one another's keepers. Out of this, we recognize the preciousness of life and the deep interconnection between body and spirit that will help us be made whole.

As a people who survived fourteen generations of slavery and seven generations of emancipation, the blending of body and soul is crucial to understanding and then constructing what the next seven generations will hold. A womanist spirituality of wholeness is founded on the belief that values like hope, virtue, sacrifice, risk, and accountability have had a different cast in the Black community.[52] The reinterpretation of these values has helped to hold Black folk in their sanity and determination.

Such values must be brought to the fore again. Our postmodern culture is breeding a kind of passivity in which the story of Black self-destruction and hatred becomes a daily item on the news wires. Black society and culture has changed and we are quickly moving away from the relational character of Black life that has sustained us and into an individualistic, nihilistic morality with no meaning-filled ethical core. This loss of values is the inheritance we gain from separating body and spirit, from placing individual over and against communal concerns.

However, in its advocacy for relationality, womanist spirituality must take care that relationality itself does not slip into the miasma of abstractions. This will lead womanist spirituality down the path of weak ethical reflection and practice.[53] A womanist spirituality measures its reflection against the backdrop of the sociohistoric reality of Black life in the United States. This means that its project is endless as it works to discover and rediscover the intricacies of African American life from past to present. This reveals a paradoxical legacy of passivity, accommodation, assimilation, and protest. The lessons learned will always be tempered by the lessons yet to come. This makes a womanist spirituality a dynamic process. In the end, we will be forced to make hard ethical choices. In a cosmos filled with worlds of oppression, we have no other option. The task of a womanist spirituality is to illuminate and question the oppression, and then begin the eradication of radical oppression and devaluation of the self and the community in the context of structural evil. Such evil operates in the interstices of human existence and in the novelty of creation. Such moral wrongness is rooted in our sociohistorical is-ness. Ultimately, we cannot accomplish this alone. Not only do we turn to our relational bonds with one another, we must also turn to the God who shapes our hands, feet, necks, and dark, dark livers.

To be called beloved is to ponder these things in our hearts that we are to grow big. Through the toxic landfills and trash heaps of everyone else's refuse, through the decades of disenfranchisement and legalized segregation, through the violence of mobs of respectable and influential folk, through skewed gender relations that beget the noose of social control—womanist spiritual reflection demands that we stand up and dance with sometimes twisted hips to the rest of what our hearts are saying. The reality of Black folk will give us the music to the song we must dance. To be called beloved is to do ethical reflection with the deeply held knowledge that we are not dipped, we are not sprinkled, we are not immersed, but we are washed in the grace of God.

CHAPTER FOUR

Writing the Right

GENDER AND SEXUALITY
IN AFRICAN AMERICAN COMMUNITY

memories so old
    time has forgot them
memories so old
    they sear my soul
memories so old
    the world has gone after
memories so old
    they wrest my heart from tomorrows

such memories cut deep
such memories die hard
such memories maim
such memories are lies
    lies
    lies

memories so old
    my spirit is like winter
memories so old
    hope doesn't fit into my vocabulary
memories so old
    crucibles of hatred surround me
memories so old
    i must find the way to dream

such memories cut deep
such memories die hard
such memories maim
such memories need a God
    of breath by breath love

We do not love ourselves. We do not love a whole holy God.

Celie's letters to God and to her sister Nettie in Alice Walker's novel *The Color Purple* are letters of self-discovery, self-examination, and self-exploration. It is a novel that tells us what happens when the missing parts of our lives are found as African American women and men in this society and culture. The fact that these are a series of letters that almost never reach their addressee is not important. The fact that the letters are sent to readers who cannot effect social change and cannot hear the voice of the writer except in the memory is immaterial. Letters, in this case, are sent to those who were long absent. What Walker tells us, in part, is that ways into the kinds of transformations these letters chronicle are not based on immediate or perhaps even visible gain. There is an element in writing letters to God that is holy and irrational. Such a spirituality as this is not based on reason alone. It is a spirituality that calls us into a deeper and newer relationship with God. This relationship, as Shug tells Celie, is intensely beyond and within who we are.

Celie is writing the right into her life as a poor, ugly Black woman who cannot be free until she begins the freedom journey herself. Her God never listens to "poor colored women," he is "big and old and tall and graybearded and white" with "white robes and bare feet, cool bluish-gray big eyes and white lashes." She is challenged to embark on this journey into a new God by her friend, mentor, and lover Shug Avery. Shug rocks Celie's understanding of God to its very core. Shug's God is never *found* in church, but a God that people bring with them to church to share with others. Shug speaks the truth about God as she knows it:

God is inside you and inside everybody else. You come into the world with God. But only them that search for it inside find it. And sometimes it just manifest itself even if you not looking, or don't know what you looking for. Trouble do it for most folks, I think. Sorrow, lord. Feeling like shit.

It? I ast.

Yeah, It. God ain't a he or a she, but a It.

But what do it look like? I ast.

Don't look like nothing, she say. It ain't a picture show. It ain't something you can look at apart from anything else, including yourself. I believe God is everything, say Shug. Everything that is or ever was or ever will be. And when you can feel that, you be happy to feel that, you've found It.[1]

Before the conversation with Shug, Celie's letters to God are monuments of passive resignation and blind faith in a benevolent, but silent God. To this God, she writes and is able to bear her abuse, pain, and suffering. Celie has a limited sense of self. However, when she learns the truth of her "lynched daddy, crazy mamma, lowdown dog of a step pa, and a sister [she] probably won't ever see again." Her God becomes like all the men she knows—"trifling, forgitful and lowdown." And she is certain that her God is asleep—and as Shug explains it, he is.

Celie's is an other-worldly eschatology in which God does not hear or liberate those who have been brutalized and raped. This is a silent God who bears our pain by allowing us to suffer our way through good works. Unfortunately, Celie's God only reifies her low self-esteem and does nothing to effect meaningful change or transformation on the individual and personal level. The church, then, becomes a place where Celie seeks to prove herself worthy of this silent God's love.

As Delores Williams notes, Celie's understanding of God resembles some of the theological views and ecclesiastical practices that have been alive in the Black community for years.[2] Further, Williams notes that her eschatology is similar to that expressed by Black slaves in some of the spirituals that claim one's relief from a life of oppression is death and going to heaven. For Williams, it is not enough that some Black churches have given up a White Jesus as savior. These same churches still hold fast to a male God. This is readily translated to maleness as divine, authoritative, and mystical. Femaleness becomes like Mr.'s description of Celie—black, poor, ugly, a woman, nothing at all.

Walker's portrayal of a passive Celie and an all too human male God readies the way for a new understanding of God for Black children, men, and women that is a pathway to a deepening spirituality and a liberating hope. In the novel, women bonding is the first step. As we broaden this to the communal context, this is a challenge for the African American community to examine the ways in which we do and do not practice and seek healthy relations as female and male. Shug teaches Celie to begin to believe in a God beyond gender, a God who is Spirit and intimately connected to the fabric of our existences. This fuller understanding of God is not dependent on human beings to be present, to care, to love, to create beauty, to live out the Spirit. This is a God of grace and grit that loves and angers, that expands our understanding of sexuality and loving, that is angered when we fail to see the beauty of creation, in ourselves, and in one another.

However, Walker is direct in her message. Our concepts of God either support the oppression of Black folk in gender-based, racist, classist constructs, or they serve as companion and confederate to our struggle for liberation and faithfulness. For Walker, and for us, a Black male God is not an improvement over a White male God; a Black or White female God offers little lasting salvation over a male God. In short, we are far too impressed with ourselves as human beings and this vanity crafts within us a God who "just sit up there glorying in being deef." Our challenge is to reach both within ourselves and without to explore the nature of the Spirit. Shug calls all of us into a spiritual awakening to a loving God who wants people of faith to celebrate life, to experience life-affirming and respecting pleasure, and gets annoyed when we fail to notice the color purple in a field.

Walker insists on the fundamentality of a spiritual life and a spirituality that seeks to bring us into community and into relationship with creation. As Celie's horizons expand, she moves from her restricted, individual world in which exploitation is daily common fare into a universe of Black folk moving into Spirit-filled tomorrows.

However, Walker's vision of God's promise is circumscribed. Celie, because she lives an interior liberation, is no threat to the social order. The rowdy and bodacious Sofia is. Sofia's story is instructive for us as well. When Sofia refuses to compromise her dignity to the White wife of the mayor, she is violently attacked, brutalized, and subdued. Sofia's liberation would require not only a new heaven, but a new earth—a radical transformation of the social and religious order. This is a warning for us as we seek to live out the spirituality of a God of the Spirit—this is dangerous and perhaps we will not all come out fully rescued from oppression. *But we must seek this Spirit.* Walker offers to us the tools of bonding—trust, respect, shared power, unconditional love. Unlike Walker's depiction of Celie's personal transformation, this only comes for us through our collective sociopolitical, theo-ethical, spiritual struggle. In short this is work that requires Baby Suggs's strong arms and big heart.

Unlike Celie, our progress cannot remain entirely in our private worlds. Too many of us are able to describe racist and sexist practices in our communities without realizing what we are describing is evil and unjust. We depend on our Sofias to live large the scandal of sexism and racism. Our knowledge is in bits and pieces scattered to the winds of injustice and we fail to develop pithy analysis or piercing historical vision to identify the substance of oppression. We must go beyond Celie's transformation of herself into a communal ring shout for justness. The reimaging of God Walker provides for us will help guide the way. New visions of God will help us into new visions of what it means for us to be female and male.

This radical reformulation of the nature of God for an oppressed Black woman is not only Celie's story, it is also Mr.'s who later gains his name, Albert. It is the story of Mr. moving from his shameful ways of degrading Celie and his children to an Albert who finds out that "meanness kill[s]" and can allow his son to hold him as he sleeps to gain respite from Celie's curse on him when she prepared to leave Mr. for Memphis with Shug. It is a story of Black women and men. As harsh as some of the telling, as painful as some of the growth, it is an African American story of moving beyond the evil finitude of sexism and heterosexism into the promise of truly greeting one another as "brother" and "sister." It *is* our story. The spirituality found in discovering a God unbound by human minds and hearts will ultimately free us from ourselves as Black men and women. But we have work to do.

SOME DON'T HAVE GOD TO SHARE

Black folk have watched, observed, and studied, the larger culture. And without even realizing it, we have taken as our own ways of relating that are often not true to our African, Native American, and Caribbean roots. Still in the 1990s, too many of us think and act as though it's "natural" if not "normal" for men to dominate due to their participation in public life and that women are relegated to the private or domestic sphere. This assignation of place gives rise to universal male authority over women and a higher valuation of male over female roles.

Within each set of social relations in U.S. society and culture, there is an imbalance of power. Hegemony maintains this inequality and is seen as normal and right. Hegemony also works to keep the dominant group in power by promoting its own worldview as neutral, universal, and moral. This works to ensure that those who do not have power see the world the way those who do have power see it. This does not (although the result often is) immediately lead to passivity. As thinking and faithful people, we have within our grasp power to question this alleged authority and challenge this violation of power and authority to continue to legitimate its actions and ideas. It is to continually pick up the rock Celie must throw every time she sees her old model of God trying to conjure itself back into a position of dominance in her life.

The public realm as we have crafted it contains the institutionalized rules and practices that define the appropriate modes of action. These are the political, economic, legal, cultural, and social institutions in which we live as a society. In addition, these are the wide range of actions and practices covered by law. The public realm is the arena of paid work and ideas. It is the world of men. This country's laws, values, education, and morality are debated and shaped in this sphere. Despite the gains made in recent years, men, not women, remain the primary participants in this sphere.

The private realm is that place of individual actions and interpersonal relations. It is the home. It is the arena where the dominant cultural norms of our society place women. Each woman lives with this split and participates in its existence *and* maintenance—African American and White. The private realm does not become a place of respite and retooling to fight injustice and advocate a fuller humanity for all peoples.

In the oppression matrix in which the public/private realm split occurs, the structural and systematic character of the social inequalities must not be lost. It is difficult to point to the specifics of oppression, particularly gender-based oppression, but there are some features that can shed light on the dimly lit corridors of injustice.[3] First, intent is not usually a factor. In other words, gender bias and discrimination is so integrated into our lives and our institutions that it becomes like breathing—present until we die. This grim reality means that it is easy for all of us to participate in oppressive practices and ideologies without consciously intending to do so.

Second, one can be oppressed without feeling oppressed. The litmus test for whether or not oppression is indeed happening *may not* necessarily be those to whom it is happening. Our human ability for denial and obfuscation cannot be underestimated as both a tool for self-preservation *and* a means for continued domination and subjugation.

Third, some women may not feel oppressed because they benefit from the status quo. The harsh reality is that there are always some benefits that are created as enticements and entitlements for those who become allies to injustice and oppression. A woman who experiences a measure of comfort and security must work with great diligence to uncover the sharp double edge of oppression and domination.

Finally, women can remain unaware of their oppression because they may see gender as the most salient part of their identity. Rather than view our femininities and masculinities as consisting of race, ethnicity, religion, class, age, and so forth, *in addition* to gender (hence the plural form of femininity and masculinity), some women may see themselves as total woman. She is who her gender is, and this gender identity is a social construction.

There are permutations when considering the impact of race in gender-based oppression. We take separate paths when we reach the juncture of the systematic exclusion of African American men (and the majority of men of color) from the public sphere of the dominant White culture. This exclusion suggests that sex-role relationships between people of color cannot be explained fully by the structural oppression between the domestic and public spheres or the differential participation of men and women in the public sphere.

Therefore, it is necessary to distinguish between the public life of the dominant and the dominated societies. The public life of the dominated society is *always* subject to the stresses put upon it by the dominant society. The private life of the dominated society suffers even more so than that of the dominant society's.

The sad irony is that African American women and men were never meant to participate as full members of this public/private split. African American women have been forced to play a highly functional and autonomous role within the family and Black society due to economic and social conditions that have devalued and ill-defined African American men and women historically.

Black women and men are warehoused, as are other women and men of color and White women, into images of womanhood and manhood imposed by a larger society. Black women also know that they will never reach this model due to the constraints of race and class. What emerges is what Annelies Knoppers terms "privileged femininity" and "hegemonic masculinity."[4]

Privileged femininity, according to Knoppers has no separate definition for any social group because it is tied to hegemonic masculinity. This means that what is desirable for women is defined in relation to what is hegemonically masculine. This femininity is, in short, constructed to accommodate the wants and interests of men. The central feature is attractiveness and beauty. This moves beyond physical appearance to include sociability and the nurture of men and children.

Femininity of privilege has many twists and turns. One such turn was a 1989 Massachusetts court case in which a woman who suffered a miscarriage in a drunk-driving accident was charged with vehicular homicide when the fetus was delivered stillborn.[5] Earlier that year, a pregnant Missouri inmate sued the state on behalf of her unborn fetus.[6] The inmate claimed that the Thirteenth Amendment prevents imprisonment of the fetus because it was not tried, charged, and sentenced. In her suit against the state of Missouri, she used Missouri's own antiabortion statute declaring that life begins at conception, to argue that such a statute affords a fetus all the rights of personhood.

These two cases serve to highlight the sometimes nuanced nature of privileged femininity. Patricia J. Williams argues that the Massachusetts case only makes sense if the litigation model employed is that of mother versus fetus.[7] She further argues that the fetus and the mother are one and that the fetus is not a separate person from the moment of conception—it is a completely interconnected part of a woman's body. Indeed for Williams, she is not sure that a child who has left the womb is really a separate person until sometime after the age of two. While I cannot go quite this far, I do believe that Williams's general argument is quite salient.

These cases point to the notion that the *idea* of the child is more important than the actual child or the actual condition of the woman of whose body the real fetus is a part. The idea of the child is pitted against the woman in both cases, and the woman's need for decent health care is suppressed in favor of what Williams calls a "conceptual entity" that is "innocent, ideal, and all potential." Privileged femininity is dangerous, for the actual needs, desires, and rights of women may well be subjugated to those of children and men.

The result of privileged femininity for Black women is a legacy of being called matriarchs, Sapphires, and castrators. This is due largely to the active role many Black women have had to play in the support of children, husbands, and Black society. All have usually assumed the Black woman's capabilities. This legacy differs considerably from where the majority of White women begin. White culture, by and large, does not assume that White women are capable. Black women who have the legacy of clearing the fields, caring for the children of others as well as their own, and functioning in marginalized roles—while being called on to provide the moral center of Black values—are considered a deviation from the norm and an anomaly.

This is more than a cruel joke of sexism. For what this does is set up a system of inequalities that stunt the mental, spiritual, emotional, social, economic, and physical growth of African American children, men, and women. We end up fighting one another and putting forth such lopsided and misogynistic views as Shahrazad Ali's *The Blackman's Guide to Understanding the Blackwoman*. The pity of this, is that Ali, a Black woman, condones emotional, physical, and spiritual battering, abuse, and violence against Black women by Black men. All this in the name of some misbegotten notion of building up African American manhood and womanhood.

Among her many observations:

> It has been proven that a Blackman is capable of taking a woman and making her beautiful, intelligent and wise. She is not able to create this same effect by herself.
>
> A good woman. The kind of woman who is in submission to her man and loves it. The kind of woman who obeys because she wants to obey and not because she is forced into doing so.[8]

Much of what Ali advocates in her book condones violence against women and children in the name of a renewed communal solidarity among Black folk.

Ali says that she has come to her conclusions based on information obtained through interviews and participant observation. What she does not tell us is the number of women interviewed, their socioeconomic status, the questions asked, or the method of interview. We, as African Americans, have often been the victims of extensive negative stereotyping and conclusions about our alleged pathology that has been based on "reports." It is no better when we are the ones who do it to ourselves. There is no future in setting up our *own* system of subjugation.

Concepts of African American manhood and womanhood have biological roots *and* emerge from socialization and acculturation. If we fail to see that we take in the culture around us in our breathing, if we miss that we are picking up all sorts of cues about what it means to be a "real" man or a "womanly" woman or a "whole" people through institutions, if we miss that we are socialized along gender lines, then we fall victim to racism and sexism.

When we lash out at one another, what we commit is horizontal violence, not nation-building. We destroy pieces of our selves, and we cut short hope for shattering the silence of sexism in the African American community. What we commit, in black face, is a pale mimicry of what too many White folks do to one another. It has functioned well to create a society built upon injustices. But it reflects neither King's dream nor Malcolm's nightmare. It reflects a broken, dispirited people who grasp at the rods of injustice rather than the branches of community. Such community can only be found in the body and souls of a people who seek to understand the nature of the curse that restrictive gender roles place on us in U.S. culture. The Black body and the Black soul become a battleground.

AND ALL THE COLORED FOLKS IS CURSED

The Black body has long been a site of contention. Herodotus spread rumors that certain parts of Africa were inhabited by a race of monstrous-looking humans.[9] Medieval art often represented Blacks as grotesque figures with thick lips, large noses, receding chins, prominent cheek bones, and curly hair.[10] By the eighteenth century, some European artists and intellectuals began to recognize the subjectivity of their own standards of beauty. However, the Black female body was an icon for Black sexuality broadly considered, and Black men and women were icons for deviant sexuality. This was played out to the degree that only certain body parts, not the whole female were displayed in the salons of Paris.

Sander L. Gilman suggests that the Black presence in early North American society allowed Whites to sexualize their world by projecting onto Blacks sexuality that was disassociated from whiteness.[11] The body of the indentured servant, Sarah Bartmann, exemplified this spectacle of female body parts. Dubbed the "Hottentot Venus," Bartmann's naked body was repeatedly displayed over a period of five years between 1810 and 1815. When she died, at the age of twenty-five, she was dissected by her admirers and in the name of science. As bell hooks considers Bartmann's story, she notes that the audience who paid to see her buttocks (that held special fascination for the spectators) and fantasize about the uniqueness of genitalia in life could now examine both in death.

In the late twentieth century, African American male filmmakers send a subtle message that Black women are unfit or questionable models of femininity. In such recent films as *Jungle Fever, Boyz N the Hood,* and *New Jack City,* Black women are portrayed as destroying the Black community by either being too attainable, incapable of parenting, or causing terminal rifts between Black men. Before these films, Black female film characters were confined to two lightweight (and often light skinned) cartoon stereotypes: whores (*Cabin in the Sky*) and good girls (*Stormy Weather*).

Contemporary films such as *Boyz N the Hood* demonize the Black mother. The viewer is told little about the mothers in this film. However visual cues are used to encourage stereotypical conclusions. The audience is never told what Tre's mother does for a living, or whether Doughboy's mother works, is on welfare, or has ever been married, we find out nothing about the single Black mother whose babies run in the street. The focus on violence against Black men obscures the world of Black women in our communities. In a sad but dangerous way, women's realities, lives, and bodies become subsidiary to guns and violence and the men who control them. Finally, the message seeps through the celluloid—those who do not have fathers fail, those who do have fathers succeed.

In real life, the bartering of Black female flesh continues. A White couple deposited the husband's sperm in a sperm bank. Later, the wife returned to be inseminated and gave birth to a Black daughter. The clinic denies that the sperm came from their bank, the woman charged the clinic with negligence and medical malpractice. For the woman, "her insemination 'became a tragedy and her life a nightmare,'" but the child's color "has nothing to do with her anguish" and she sued when the "racial taunting of her child became unbearable."[12] There may well be legions of Black mothers and fathers who would sue, if they thought it feasible, to compensate their daughters' and sons' status as victims of prejudice.

Black masculinity also suffers from the iconography of Black bodies. Black men, in the United States, are portrayed as failures or as dangerous psychosexual maniacs. As a collective body, Black men have not done adequate analysis and critique of the dominant culture's norms of masculine identity. However, they have had to rework these norms to suit their social location.[13] Although the noted Black sociologist Robert Staples argues that Black males are in conflict with the normative definition of masculinity, he does not go on to stress that this conflict has never assumed the form of complete rebellion. Staples accepts hegemonic masculinity and, in doing so, fails to see or to explore how Black men could assert meaningful agency by repudiating the norms that white culture imposes on them.

However, African American men are beginning to challenge the domination of hegemonic masculinity for Black men. Both Michael Eric Dyson and Cornel West are two voices pointing the way.[14] Dyson casts a measured look at rap music and the image of Black bodies found in some of the lyrics.[15] Rap music and rap culture in general can provide a healthy and creative alternative to destructive behavior among African American juveniles in the inner city. Space, which is at a premium, can be created by words and not physical and emotional violence.

However, groups such as 2 Live Crew belie assumptions about women as exclusive objects of male sexual satisfaction. Dyson notes that 2 Live Crew's sexism brings to light the "subterranean, pornographic fantasies of men in a patriarchal culture that thrives on strategies of domination in infinitely adaptable guises, including racial, sexual, and class domination."[16] For Dyson, the double standard of explicit denial and secret permission are the bedrock of sexism, for this standard obfuscates guilt and complicity so that the practice of sexism flourishes. He notes:

> Black men have not by and large been able to set the political, economic, and social terms that regulate women's lives, we have often victimized black women with a form of sexist, machismo-laden behavior that compensated for debilitating forms of social emasculation under the sting of racism. . . . Black communities must begin facing up to the lethal consequences of our own sexism.[17]

For Dyson, 2 Live Crew brings to the surface the repressed U.S. cultural attitudes toward Black male sexuality that are a "sordid range of stereotypes, jealousies, fears [that have] developed around black men wielding their sexuality in ways that are perceived as untoward, unruly, or uncontrolled."[18] In short, Black male sexual activity has often been viewed as inherently vulgar and dangerous when not directed toward Black women. Yet few questions or objections are raised about a cultural and social attitude that grants men permission to intrude on and violate

Black women's bodies. When a young White woman was gang raped by several Black and Hispanic youths in New York City's Central Park, a public outcry arose. When a Black woman was gang raped on the roof of a New York City building and thrown three stories off the building a few days after the Central Park incident, the press gave scant coverage and it was not made a police priority investigation.

LISTENING LONG ENOUGH TO TELL YOU WHAT TO DO

The reality of Black bodies as icons points the way to the fact that this is a sexually repressive culture although the media, the church, and even our personal observations may indicate that we are promiscuous. We are sexually repressed in the sense that we have made all kinds of compromises regarding our sexuality to live on this planet and in our society and to survive in the church. We live in a sexually repressive culture because even in the face of a life-denying disease like AIDS, countless folk remain ignorant of how it is transmitted, how to protect ourselves from spreading or catching the HIV virus, or even realize that everyone needs to take precautions.

I was stunned when a young woman told me that before this "AIDS thing" she had no animosity toward gays, but now she thinks *they* are a menace to society. When I asked if she were practicing safe sex, she did not know what that was. She was not aware of the need for condoms or of avoiding oral contact with the penis, vagina, or rectum. She was not aware that the use of intravenous drugs by her sexual partner who shares needles or even her sharing needles put her in the risk group for AIDS. She was unaware of the risk she runs in being sexually active without proper precautions, even in light of the growing number of heterosexuals contracting the virus. She never considered abstinence.

We are sexually repressed while at the same time being sexually active, and this is a dangerous combination. We don't understand how our bodies function or how the bodies of our sexual partners function. We fumble in the dark regarding subjects like teenage pregnancy. Time and again children repeat the all too familiar litany, "I never thought it would happen to me"; and when asked if they were using any form of birth control the answer is a resounding no. That is a manifestation of sexual repression.

We separate our bodies from our spirits in this sexual repression. We have inherited this separation from years of church doctrine and theological treatises. The history of our society and the church is one that neglects, ignores, or denigrates the body. The history is that the body is lower than the mind, which represents spirit. To be religious means living and acting in split bodies. Therefore, sexual activity is equated with sexuality. And we are to only express our sexuality within the bounds of marriage.

This is a false equation. Our sexuality is who we are as thinking, feeling, and caring human beings. It is our ability to love and nurture. To express warmth and compassion. It is not only our gonads. Heterosexism encourages the objectification of our bodies—male and female. One of its strongest underlying premises is that the emotion expressed in same-sex relationships is only that of pure sex. Too often we do not see or want to discover the care and nurture that lesbians and gay men can and do have for each other. We must raise some exacting questions about an ethic that insists that homosexuals should either try to engage in heterosexual relationships unhappily or remain celibate. An ethic is suspicious when it allows some to impose on others obligations that they are unwilling to accept for themselves.

Recognizing that we are fighting history and tradition, it is easier to see that much of the response we have, as well as others have, to gay men and lesbians comes from a subtle and deadly unwillingness to reexamine Black femininity and masculinity. This also means we fail to recognize or challenge hegemonic masculinity with its drive for power that represses, domination that subordinates, and control that berates and is abusive—physically, emotionally, spiritually. We do not recognize or challenge privileged femininity that takes its cues from the domination of hegemonic masculinity—the feminine is absolutely everything the masculine is not and serves as cheerleader for a masculinity that runs roughshod over the humanity of us all.

We cannot hear Robert E. Penn's cry—no, *demand*—of his friend Spider:

And I am tired of shame, guilt and despair. I'm afraid of dying alone. I need your help, and I don't want the fact that I'm homosexual to get in the way. . . . My medical treatment is expensive. I get upset that pharmaceutical companies are making such large profits off people with a life-threatening condition. Few insurance companies cover HIV-positive people, and my policy won't pay for essential tests for alternative therapies.[19]

Heterosexism's continued dominance means the devaluation of people. It permits the social, political, economic, and theological systems that encourage us to deny parts of our being for the sake of others, to continue to destroy all of us.

It prevents us from addressing fully sexism *and* racism. The 1992 report from the President's Commission on AIDS alarmed many. The idea that 21 percent of the total population accounts for 46 percent of the people in the U.S. living with AIDS caught many off guard.[20] African Americans constitute 12 percent of the United States population and nearly 30 percent of AIDS cases. Hispanics/Latinos constitute 9 percent of the population and 17 percent of the AIDS cases. The 1993 numbers continue to rise with Blacks and Hispanics/Latinos accounting for 48 percent of the reported AIDS cases. The increase for Blacks to a firm 31 percent of the cases is the cause.

The 1989 age-adjusted HIV-related death rate among Black males was three times that of White males. African American females were nine times more likely to die of HIV than White females. The Commission believes that the trends suggest that this disproportionate impact is likely to continue. This means that by 1995 in the U.S., the percentage of youths who have been or will be left orphaned by the HIV epidemic will be 17 percent of children and 12 percent of adolescents. To give you an idea of the numbers, in 1991 32,400 children, adolescents, and young adults were orphaned by AIDS. By 1995, the estimates run from 72,000 to 80,700. By 2000, the estimates are 125,000 to 146,000.[21]

It is important to note that Native Americans and Asian Americans/Pacific Islanders are underrepresented among AIDS cases in proportion to their numbers in the total population. In 1992, Asian American/Pacific Islanders were 3 percent of the population and 0.6 percent of the AIDS cases. Native Americans were 0.8 percent of the population and 0.17 percent of the reported AIDS cases. However, from 1989 to 1990, the number of Native American AIDS cases increased faster than cases among any other racial/ethnic group.

The African American community is the most disproportionately represented with respect to HIV/AIDS. Beginning in 1990, AIDS became the leading cause of death for Black men between the ages of 35 and 44 and the second leading cause of death for Black men and women between the ages of 25 and 36. Of the AIDS cases, 78 percent are adult men (13 years or older), 19 percent are adult women, and 3 percent are pediatric (children younger than 13 years).

For African American men, homosexual contact accounts for 43 percent of the cases, injection drug use accounts for 36 percent, men who have sex with men and also inject drugs are 7 percent, the remaining 14 percent are presumed heterosexual with no injection drug use.

For African American women, 53 percent of AIDS cases in adult women are from injection drug use. Heterosexual contact with an injection drug user accounts for 21 percent, and 6 percent are due to heterosexual contact with a HIV-infected person who is not an injection drug user.

Black children have accounted for 54 percent of all the reported pediatric AIDS cases in the nation. Ninety-four percent have been due to perinatal transmissions from mothers infected with HIV. Four percent have been due to hemophilia-related blood products or the receipt of an HIV-contaminated blood tranfusion. The mode of the remaining 2 percent cannot be determined.

However, in 1987 the statistics were already alarming. Then, Blacks and Hispanics made up 20 percent of the population. At a conference, I raised the concern that the Black community was under siege with AIDS because even then, 37 percent of the male AIDS sufferers and 73 percent of the female sufferers were Black or Hispanic. I was told by several Black folk in attendance that using such statistics was detrimental to the Black community. Their concern was the *perception* that the folks who had contracted the HIV virus were gay men or prostitutes. They could not hear that the disproportionate rise of AIDS in our communities is due to intravenous drug use. Yes, there are Black gay men who contract HIV/AIDS and die. But there are Black men and women like Arthur Ashe and Ruby Johnson who die of the complications of AIDS. Fear of an image or images *will* literally kill us if we do not address the realities.

CONJURING UP BIG ROCKS

The heterosexism in our communities continues to allow too many to believe that if they are not gay men, then they do not have to worry. This, in spite of the fact that the highest levels of knowledge among Black folks were found in the younger groups and in those with the most education. Television, newspapers, magazines, and radio are acting as helpful resources for the African American community. It is not that we do not know how AIDS is transmitted; as a community, we do. But this contrasts with the fact that only 14 percent of African Americans have been tested.

We are sexually repressed and sexually active and we are getting ourselves in trouble. Among high school students, 60 percent of the African American males and 20 percent of the females reported having had four or more sex partners. Only 55 percent of the males and 37 percent of the females reported having used a condom during their most recent intercourse. In a survey of sixteen to nineteen year olds, only 28 percent reported always using a condom. This, even though the 1993 Centers for Disease Control figures show that the number of AIDS cases increased most rapidly among heterosexuals—especially young people and Black and Hispanic/Latino women. This increase was 130 percent more than 1992: 4,045 to 9,288.[22]

The increase is greater among women than men and higher among Blacks and Hispanics/Latinos than among Whites. The largest increases were among teenagers and young adults—primarily through heterosexual transmission.

Meanwhile, there is still no systematic, structural, and effective anti-drug program in communities of the dispossessed in this nation. The spiritual reimaging of God as Spirit that Shug challenges us with is a moral and spiritual call to do justice toward our bodies, our sexuality, and our genders. It is justice that tells us that each of us has worth, each of us has the right to have that worth recognized and respected, each of us has a right to be known for who we are. Justice holds us accountable to and with one another.

If Black folk cannot live into justice or help create it, then we have consigned ourselves to worthlessness. For to continue in pathways in which we condone or ignore the violence we do to our minds, bodies, and souls is to allow racism, sexism, and heterosexism to dictate to us our values and our aspirations. We must make it personal and communal, our struggle for justice.

It is out of this milieu that African Americans must begin to have open and honest conversations about how sexism and heterosexism destroys the fabric of a community that is literally holding on for dear life in this nation. Too many of us carry within us the scenes of battering and pillage to our souls and bodies. Too many of us have been there or heard about the times someone thought "No" meant "Yes." Too many of us have shaken our heads when we heard sounds during the night or during the day. Too many of us have been at the checkout counter and chatted with a checker who was wearing a black eye for the fourth or fifth time. And in our souls we wanted to say something, but we saw in her eyes, "Don't ask." Make no mistake about what sexism and heterosexism do to the soul and spirit. For much of what spawns the ability to commit violence to a physical body or to view the body as sexual icon is also that which holds racism and classism in place. It is a deep and abiding desire and then ability to dominate, to control, to dehumanize, to devalue. It is an abomination to the very fiber of existence.

African Americans must take this into the communal context. Our self-respect, our self-esteem, our future as a people is under assault. And in too many cases and all too often, we are leading our attackers. It is not only what racism has done to us, it is not only what sexism has done to us, it is not only what heterosexism and all the other "isms" have done to us. When Shug talks about a God of creation, and we begin to envision a spirituality of a whole, holy God, we must, as African American people of faith, recognize that it is what we do to ourselves; it is how we respond to the structural injustices of this day. We need to get clear on why and how we permit and commit sexual violence on Black folk. We need to decide how we are going to love ourselves and one another rather than rely on popular culture, even our own popular culture, to tell us who we have been, who we are, and where we are heading, and how we are to behave with one another in justice and hope.

We need to hear again "separate but equal." And this time, expand the notion of what it means to be separate in this culture. Too often when we talk about separating ourselves, we are actually setting someone up as a target. When cast in the context of sexism and heterosexism, it can mean beating someone into invisibility, into silence, into despair. There is no equality here. There is no justice. There is no equity. There is no fairness.

The rock Celie conjures to chase away a God who is deaf to our cries of anguish and alienation, shatters our ignorance of the death-dealing consequences of hegemonic masculinity and privileged femininity—sexism and heterosexism. For far too long, the Black community had to battle the image that sexual and domestic violence were confined to our communities. Years ago, I remember quite clearly having to repeat the litany that violence of this sort is not confined to folks living in poverty or to specific communities of racial/ethnic folk. What we did, unwittingly, is not focus enough on what *was* and *is* going on that condones and commits sexual and domestic violence among Black people.

Picking up Celie's rock to chase away a moribund God of aloofness means that African American Christians must shape our identities as a faithful community seeking wholeness in a God who is the essence of creation *for ourselves*. Yes, we are male and female, young, middle-aged, old, conservative, neoconservative, liberal, radical, nationalist, patriotic, anarchist. Yes we come in a variety of colors and shapes, we have diversity of sexualities, we are a variety of religions, and we have a multitude of ways to express ourselves in the arts. What we cannot afford is to have no clue about who we are. For you can be sure that someone or some industry will be more than happy to define us to suit their purposes, their gain, their profit—not ours. We must do this for ourselves as individuals and our collective selves as a people. If we can do this, we will begin to look at the structural and emotional roots of violence in our community.

We have a responsibility for our future. We must decide if we are going to live in an uneasy, destructive, but comfortable acquiescence or in communal accountability. Are we going to live with some of us filling the role of colonized victims? Or are we going to realize the great gift of who we are as African Americans and begin to "git man off [our] eyeball" so that we can see a God whose spirit calls us into a spirituality that loves our bodies into wholeness as God holds us in the palm of creation and with creation itself. We owe one another respect and the right to our dignity as people of God. If we deny justice and continue to condone Black versions of sexism and heterosexism to guide our faith communities and our social lives, we are telling some of our community that they are worthless. As people of faith, we must teach and live gender justice. We must engage in community building work that ministers to our souls, lifts our spirits (individually and collectively), assures our connection with one another and to God, pulls us beyond ourselves. The Black religious community needs to create large spaces of welcome, understanding, and confrontation from the pulpit to its religious programming. Folk need to hear the church say in a clear and unequivocal voice that sexual and domestic violence are not acceptable behaviors but they are lethal values.

Black folk need to work with Black folk to help to create positive images of male and female that are not dominated by someone else's version of who we are. We must become one another's harvest and in doing so, we will begin to recognize the gift of life we have in one another and turn away from battering ourselves into victimage. One place to begin to gain these new images is in the life of a church that no longer condones business as usual, that transmits religiosized versions of domination and subordination.

Justice holds us accountable to the demands of living in a community of responsibility and one that fosters self-worth and self-esteem for others and for itself. Every time we walk into a dessert shop and see gigantic chocolate breasts complete with nipples and think of how funny this is and how good the chocolate must be, every time we watch *School Daze* or *Boyz N the Hood* and miss *Daughters of the Dust* or *Losing Ground,* every time we hear the sounds during the night or day, every time we *feel* someone we know or don't know is in trouble, every time we see injustice and treat it as just—we have done violence and mayhem to the body and soul. We have pushed ourselves away from the pulse of morning and condemned ourselves to "the gloom of dust and ages."[23]

WE COME INTO THE WORLD WITH GOD

Shug's God in and of creation calls us to recreate our material and spiritual homes. The spirituality of a God feeling our pulse with joy and sorrow calls each of us to move beyond the narrow confines of social constructions of gender that imprison and maim. Alice Walker's *The Color Purple* can serve as a guide to this journey. A spirituality that seeks to help us love ourselves and a whole and holy God moves us beyond the narrow confines of hegemonic masculinity and privileged femininity into a *community* of children, men, and women. The *production* of images of Black bodies is politically charged and spiritually moribund.

Of the numerous lessons found in Walker's novel, we must not lose sight of the transformation of Mr. into Albert and Celie into Miss Celie. Walker's work, not Steven Spielberg's movie version, deals with complex interpersonal transformations of Black female and male roles and expectations. Spielberg painted a simple stereotypical version of Black manhood (threatening and dangerous) in which Albert's conversion from a violent male chauvinist to a compassionate caring person wanes into obscurity.

This is not the image nor the vision of the spirituality of the novel. The home that Celie and Albert create for themselves is rooted in Celie's conversion to the God who is in creation, listening intently and passionately to the injustices and justices we do. This God is a Creator of life as art and gift. This God is the one who seeks justice for even "poor colored women" and men and children. This is a God who encompasses all of our racial/ethnic identities, our sexualities, our classes, our religious traditions, our abilities—our is-ness—and wills with us a home of health and nurture for people seeking to shatter the confines of destructive gender roles and identities.

This will not come without cost or upheaval. The hope that Walker presents us with is that we may well, if we choose to seek the Spirit, have the will to dare the injustices and stereotypes to cocreate ourselves in a liberative image of God.

CHAPTER FIVE

Another Kind of Poetry

IDENTITY AND COLORISM IN BLACK LIFE

> *slavery is not dead*
> *even behind the cold iron bars of*
> > *the prisons*
> > *there are tensile threads of color and beauty*
> *wrapped tight around the neck*
> > *these threads choke the life*
> > *out of our dignity*
> *at least we see the prison bars*
> > *how perfect their power*
> > *to entrap and enslave a*
> > *whole generation*
> *we cannot see the tensile threads*
> > *only feel their deadly pressure*
> > *on our necks*

It is odd indeed for a Black woman to begin to find her spiritual and social identity in the midst of luxury, ease, and a cruise. This is where Avey Johnson, the protagonist in Paule Marshall's *Praisesong for the Widow,* begins her journey home to her Caribbean roots, African heritage, and an integrated African American life. This amalgam of identities is essential for the relatively successful and somewhat assimilated Black middle class in the United States. The elderly women on the boat to Carriacou, the androgynous Lebert Joseph, and the memory of her Aunt Cuney's recitations join forces to help Avey reclaim her lost cultural heritage. This heritage seeped away from her and her husband, Jay (later Jerome), as they slowly, but surely, bent under years of cultural hegemony to assimilate into a restrictive and death-bringing society.

Praisesong highlights a pestilent conflict of values between the material ones of the dominant culture in the U.S. and the spiritual ones of an oppressed group. If spiritual values or spirituality involves the living of one's life in integrity and faithfulness in God, then this clash represents the imposition of societal restraints by the dominant culture that ultimately demands a denial of ethnic and racial identity to succeed. Joyce Pettis notes that the "problems between American middle-class economic status and retention of cultural values important to African Americans" are constant themes in Marshall's fiction.[1]

SOME LINEN BURIAL CLOTHES LYING IN A HEAP

Avey's "good life" Caribbean vacation cruise in the West Indies is disrupted when she is unable to eat a rich parfait and has a dream about her great-aunt Cuney. Marshall's symbolism is clear and direct. The parfait represents the overabundance that is consonant with a cruise and Avey's "vague bloated feeling" like a "huge tumor."[2] The tumorous reaction to the over-rich food is symptomatic of Avey's spiritual malaise in which the White faces of the cruise become images of skeletons and the shot skeet becomes a dying wounded bird. In revealing her decision to leave the cruise and return to the safety of North White Plains to her two friends, her friend Thomasina proves prophetic: "A person would have to have a reason for doing a thing like this. No, somethin's deep behind this mess."[3]

Deep it is. Before Avey can leave the cruise, her Aunt Cuney appears before her at Ibo Landing in Tatem, South Carolina. As she mutely begs Avey to come with her to again experience and respect the ritual of their communal heritage, her passivity turns to pleading. In the ensuing struggle, Avey's stole (representative of her materialistic, middle-class existence) was trampled underfoot. This battle between spiritual and material leaves Avey in denial as she can remember the force of Aunt Cuney's hand on her wrist, but she does not analyze her dream. Yet the unnamed bothers her.

Avey must wait a day in Grenada for the next plane. In her hotel room her memories move to her Brooklyn tenement on Halsey Street with its poverty and its joys. She begins by recalling the joys: rituals involving jazz, blues, and poetry. These rituals and cultural markers brought delight into Avey's and Jay's early marriage. Their rich and holy sexual lives were surrounded by the African female deities Yemoja and Oya and the Haitian Erzulie Frieda. She then places these joys in their context—

poverty, hunger, and despair. Jay overcomes the odds and improves his family's lives economically at a tragic cost. The family loses its rituals and stories of their heritage through neglect. The children become solemn and the trips to Tatem cease.

For Avey, Jay is now "Jerome Johnson" who builds their lives materially, not spiritually. However, Jay is not the villain, but the victim. He survives an oppressive social order by paying with his spirit so that his family can exist. Avey sees her warm memories of Halsey Street as an act of betrayal to Jay who could not remember the health and joy they shared in the midst of fear and poverty. At Jay's funeral, Avey sees the thin-lipped, colorless face of a White man superimposed on Jay's face. The control of White hegemony was complete at death. Avey realizes the life-giving qualities of their long-abandoned spirit-filled rituals.

As she stands on the wharf waiting for a taxi, the different poetry of the *patois* she hears conjures up the cadences of Tatem. In her tourist hotel room, Avey begins her middle passage back to her heritage and her spirit as she begins to estimate the cost of moving into a Black middle-class existence that is sterile. The Caribbean is perhaps the only place that she can begin to reconstruct her spirituality. Unlike the peculiar institution of the United States, slavery in the Caribbean allowed the survival of African cultural traditions. The majority of island plantations were extremely large. This meant that most slaves had little contact with their White owners and African family, cultural, and societal systems remained virtually intact.[4]

Avey's meeting with Joseph Lebert leads her on an excursion to the out-island of Carriacou where she joins her heritage and begins to integrate her spirituality into an abundant lifestyle. It is the passage from Grenada to Carriacou that is transformative—death to grace. Responding to the rocking of the boat, Avey's semiconscious dream state carries her to an Easter sermon of her youth. In the sermon, the Reverend Morrissey (a "large ruddy mulatto man with great rawboned wrists and hands and a pair of restless feet that kept him stalking the pulpit") showers the congregation with the Mark 16 account of the resurrection with strangled screams stolen from a blues singer, God's cosmic laughter, song, and embodying the "wrathful Jehovah of the Israelites."[5] For Avey, the voice from the pulpit had become God's voice that was relentless in calling out the giant stones that buried spirits, hearts, minds, and salvation. These were the stones of selfishness, hypocrisy, lying, cheating, stealing, jealousy, envy, and hate. These stones also included self-righteousness, pride, badmouthing, backbiting, small-mindedness, and malice. Reverend Morrissey called forth the stones of indifference to suffering, infidelity, false values, and acquisition. As she recalls the desperate violence of her becoming sick in church, she looses an actual explosion of vomit and diarrhea in the boat. She begins a purification ritual of cleansing, healing, and laying on of hands as the section, "*Lavé Tête,*" indicates. Through the ministrations of Lebert Joseph, the older women on the boat, and the cleansing bath from Joseph's daughter Rosalie, Avey takes the first step into a full spirituality by acknowledging her place in the diaspora.

The final section of the novel, "The Beg Pardon," refers to the ritual of ancestor reverence that is so important to West African religious worldviews and is an important link for Avey to return to her Aunt Cuney's memories and stories, to return to her heritage, and ultimately to herself. Her transformation is nearly complete as she remembers that it is more than important to remember to say her name is "Avey, short for Avatara" so that the richness and fullness of who she is, is not consumed by the dominant culture that would rob her of her full name and replace it with a circumscribed one. The Nation Dance completes the transformation—heritage, spirit, and mission are the grace that gives her new life. Avey's transformation becomes a communal one as she accepts that her knowledge of transforming tragedy into beauty must be conveyed to others—even, if not especially, in the midst of affluence. She returns home with a greater knowledge of her life as one in community and spirit. She becomes the beneficiary of grace who must then prepare this generation and those beyond for a healthy confrontation with the oppression and the alienation of their lives.

SUFFERING UNDER AN INDIFFERENT PONTIUS PILATE

Black. Deeply stained with dirt; soiled, dirty foul. . . . Having dark or deadly purposes, malignant; pertaining to or involving death, deadly, baneful, disastrous, sinister. . . . Foul, iniquitous, atrocious, horrible, wicked. . . . Indicating disgrace, censure, liability to punishment, etc.[6]

The tragedy of Jay's lost seity and the fruition of Avatara's transformed spirituality point to the importance of African American identity in an integrated spirituality. Identity helps maintain cultural continuity and wholeness in a context of oppression and injustice. The systematic assault on Black identity is centuries old. It began, in part, with the interaction of the British with West Africa and the subsequent slave trade. This brought Europeans in frequent contact with dark Africans. The British could not understand the coloring of these folk because of the universal assumption that humanity stemmed from one source. This assumption was held in place by force of church and the interpretation of Scripture. As early as 1614, the Reverend Samuel Purchas gave the following description:

> The tawney Moore, blacke Negro, duskie Libyan, ash-colored Indian, olive-coloured American, should with the whiter European become *one sheep-fold,* under *one great Sheepheard,* till *this mortalitie being swallowed up of Life,* wee may all *be one, as he and the father are one . . .* without any more distinction of Colour, Nation, Language, Sexe, Condi-
> · tion, all may be *One* in him that is One, *and only blessed for ever.*[7]

From this more hopeful stance, the legacy moved to one that conditioned us to hate and to fear black as evil and illegal. Black skin indicated intellectual and moral inferiority. This warped perception of color is what Delores Williams calls "white racial narcissism," [8] which expresses itself in an inordinate concern for White power and control. The result is thousands of Jerome Johnsons—exploited Black people considered less than and wearing ill-fitting masks of Whiteness that eventually annihilate. This form of White hegemony disregards human actions and laws when considering the rights of Black folk. It is the:

> Overvaluation of one group's skin color to the pathological point of using that group's power and authority to persecute others who are not of that skin color. . . . White racial narcissism indicates a malfunction in the American national psyche that can ultimately lead the culture to self-destruct or can lead the powerful racially narcissistic group to genocide members of a less powerful racial group.[9]

In the United States context, this began with the early settlers who frequently contrasted themselves with Blacks by using the term *Christian* more frequently than *English.* Being English and being Christian became so intertwined that the Virginia Assembly of 1670 declared that "noe negroe or Indian though baptised and enjoyned their owne Freedome shall be capable of any such purchase of christians, but yet not debarred from buying any of their owne nation."[10] After 1680, a new term appeared—White.[11] To be Christian meant to be civilized, British, and White. Rather than a term that signaled the unifying spirituality of the gospel, it was used to denote a fortress mentality that pitted White against Colored.

The Virginia code of 1705 used *Christian* much more like a definition of race than of religion:

> And for a further christian care and usage of all christian servants, *Be it so enacted, by the authority aforesaid, and it is hereby enacted,* That no negroes, mulattos, or Indians, although christians, or Jews, Moors, Mahometans, or other infidels, shall, at any time, purchase any christian servant, nor any other, except of their own complexion, or such as are declared slaves by this act.[12]

In 1753, the Virginia slave code still defined slavery in terms of religion although slavery had been based on racial, not religious difference, for several generations. Somehow, Christianity became linked with complexion.

The British borrowed the terms *Indian* and *Negro* from the Spanish. The former derived from a mistake in geographic location, the other from human complexion. When referring to Indians, the English colonists either used the proper name or called them savages. Unlike their usage of the term *Christian* with Black Africans, the British only occasionally referred to themselves as Christians and with the passage of time, dropped this and simply used the designation of English for themselves vis-à-vis Indians. Slaves were not called heathens, pagans, or savages, but Negroes, Blacks, and Africans.

During the 1700s a shift in terminology occurred such that the common term *Christian* was replaced at midcentury with the terms *English* and *free*. Skin color became an independent rationale for enslavement. Winthrop Jordan proposes that the diminished reliance on *Christian* suggests a gradual muting of the specifically religious element caused by a move toward a secular nationality.[13] This may be because African assimilation, increased slave trade, and the arrival of larger numbers of Europeans outside England prompted the colonists to turn to physiognomic differences. It seems as though religious difference was *initially* more important than color. This does not mean there was a change in the justification of slavery from religion to race. Rather, it is more likely that the colonists' initial sense of difference from the Negro was based on several pejorative qualities that associated appearance and religion. With the influx of other competing factors, race became the distinctive marker.

Nevertheless, colonists continued to seek the explanation for the dark skin of the Africans. The answer turned to most consistently was the sun. It was assumed that the sun scorched the skin, drew the bile, or blackened the blood. The British expansionists sometimes described the African sun as a curse "of such putrifying qualities, that it rotted the coates of their backs." The association of Black folks' color with the sun was commonplace in Elizabethan literature.[14] This theory simply did not explain the fact that people living along the same longitude and latitude in the Americas did not have the same dark skin of equatorial inhabitants in Africa.

By the mid-1500s, it became apparent that Indians living in the hottest regions could not be described as Black. This climatic explanation of skin color simply did not explain reality. To follow this explanation to its logical conclusion meant that once Africans were in the northern countries they should start to lose their dark color. If it did not happen in the first generation of folks, it should appear in their offspring. By the mid-1600s, this explanation paled as Blacks in Europe and the northern parts of the Americas did not whiten noticeably.

Yet there were many other British who were certain that Blackness was permanent and innate. In 1646, the physician Sir Thomas Browne hypothesized that Blackness was permanent and transmitted by the sperm. He was not sure why this was so, however. In 1695, Jordan quotes an essayist's description of Africans as "plain, their colour and wool are innate, or seminal from their first beginning"[15] in describing Black men with woolly hair.

Overall, the 1600s displayed little progress on the scientific problem of the dark color of African skin. When the 1700s dawned, the mood was one of puzzlement and wild speculation posing as scientific theorems. Early in the eighteenth century, many mixed Scripture, observation, and speculation. White interpretation of biblical stories fed into the subordination of Blackness and Black people. Genesis 9:20-27 and Amos 9:7 became popular verses that "explained" Black inferiority.[16] Thankfully as the century wore on, these explanations began to lose their popularity. However, philosophers continued to turn to sun theories and Georges Buffon thought Blacks would become perceptibly lighter by the eighth, tenth, or twelfth generation. Few were willing to go as far as John Atkins, a naval surgeon, who wrote in 1735 in his *A Voyage to Guinea, Brasil, and the West Indies; In His Majesty's Ships, the Swallow and Weymouth,* "tho' it be a little Heterodox, I am persuaded the black and white Race have, *ab origine,* sprung from different-coloured first Parent."[17] It was possible to explain African complexion by basing it on separate creations of people in distinct colors. Yet few wished to venture into such heterodox claims.

After the mid-1600s, some writers abandoned the larger questions of color to explore the more manageable one of the physiology of skin color. Marcello Malpighi's pioneering work in microscopic anatomy (1648–94) is a marker for the common view that Black skin contained a black fluid. The researchers were undaunted when they were unable to find such a substance. Although not representative of the majority opinion in the colonies, Dr. John Mitchell of Urbanna, Virginia, announced that Black skin was no different from White skin—it was thicker and denser and contained more particles. He emphasized the fundamental sameness of people of diverse appearances. For him, Negroes, Indians, and Whites were different only in the "Degree of one and the same Colour."[18]

All these theories and many subsequent White hegemonic theories were based on the common assumption that the original color of humans was white. Therefore, Blackness was a *degeneration* from the original color. The idea of degeneration from primitive Whiteness was seemingly confirmed by the fact that Black babies were born considerably lighter than their later skin color. Some, like Cornelis de Pauw, invented "facts" that they were not able to discover. In 1770, de Pauw announced that the Negro had dark brains, blood, semen and the mulatto's intermediate color was caused by the blending of dark and white semen.

The 1758 edition of Carolus Linneaus' *Systema Naturae* was foundational in the natural sciences for many subsequent pseudoscientific explanations of race and ethnicity. Linneaus developed four categories for the species "Homo": African, American, Asiatic, and European. The African was described as black, phlegmatic, relaxed, hair black, frizzled, skin silky, nose flat, lips tumid, women's bosom a matter of modesty, breasts give milk abundantly, crafty, indolent, negligent, anoints himself with grease, governed by caprice. The American was described as red, choleric, erect, black hair straight and thick, wide nostrils, freckled face, scanty beard, obstinate, content, free, paints himself with fine red lines, regulated by habit. The Asiatic was yellow, melancholy, rigid, black hair, dark eyes, severe, haughty, covetous, covered with loose garments, governed by opinions. The European was characterized as white, sanguine, brawny, hair abundantly flowing, blue eyes, gentle, acute, inventive, covered with close vestments, governed by customs. It is indeed curious that the African was the only one in which women or their breasts are mentioned.

Johann Friedrich Blumenbach, an anthropologist, brought the aesthetic criteria and cultural ideals of Greece to the fore. Like Linneaus, he held that all humans belonged to the same species and races were varieties within that species. His 1775 work, *De Generis Humani Varietate Nativa,* carried four species that moved to five in the 1781 edition, and the 1795 edition finally introduced precise language including the term *Caucasian.*[19] In each edition, Blumenbach praised the symmetrical, White face as the most beautiful of human faces because it approximated the "divine" works of Greek art. He believed that this was yoked to climate—the more moderate the climate, the more beautiful the face. It is clear where this left Africans on Blumenbach's beauty scale.

Two popular and influential pseudosciences, phrenology and physiognomy, evidenced the European-biased character of scientific speculation. The bias was built from classical aesthetic and cultural ideals. Not surprisingly, many of these race theorists were trained as artists and writers and sought to promote a love for classical antiquity to young artists and sculptors.

Phrenology, the reading of skulls, had its most notable proponent in Pieter Camper, a Dutch anatomist, who discovered the facial angle in the 1770s. The facial angle permitted comparison of human heads by using cranial and facial measurements. The ideal facial angle was 100 degrees—achieved only by the ancient Greeks. Since a beautiful face, body, nature, character, and soul were inseparable, phrenology helped establish the "natural" superiority of the Europeans who had a 97-degree angle and the "natural" inferiority of Black people who were between 60 and 70 degrees—closer to the measurements of apes and dogs.

Later, in the early 1800s, Dr. Samuel Morton claimed that the human skull size determined the character of a person's intelligence *and* moral fiber.[20] Morton and other phrenologists claimed that because White people's skulls were larger than all others and Blacks had smaller skulls, Whites were "naturally" superior to Blacks on intellectual and moral levels. Further, Morton claimed to provide documented proof that Blacks in ancient Egypt had been slaves. Therefore, Blacks had spent their entire existence on earth as slaves of the more intelligent races.

Johann Kasper Lavater, the father of physiognomy or the reading of faces, explicitly acknowledged that the art of painting was what informed his new discipline. Physiognomy equated visible physical characteristics with character and capacity. Lavater theorized that classical ideas of beauty, proportion, and moderation regulated the classification and ranking of human groups. He believed that Greek statues were models of beauty: blue eyes, horizontal forehead, bent back, round chin, short brown hair. Incidentally, these all parallel Camper's beautiful person.

Physiognomy was influential between scientists and artists. Goethe helped Lavater edit and publish his physiognomic formulations, and Sir Walter Scott and others popularized them in novels. The striking thing about the method of this discipline is that it did not rely on detailed measurements, but the visual glance. Lavater was quite clear in his instructions, "Trust your first quick impression, for it is worth more than what is usually called observation."[21] He also developed an elaborate theory of noses that associated Roman and Greek noses with conquerors and persons of refinement and taste.

Major intellectual figures of the Enlightenment accepted these ideas without having to put forward their own arguments to justify them. In the Age of Criticism, this was quite odd for those who held reason and rationale on a sublime plane to accept uncritically the authority of naturalists, anthropologists, physiognomists, and phrenologists.

Montesquieu made remarks about Blacks that seemed to suggest an ambiguous disposition toward some of these theories in his *Spirit of the Laws*. Although he opposed slavery, he did turn to the sun theory to explain the existence of slavery because "there are countries where the excess of heat enervates the body, and renders men so slothful and dispirited that nothing but the fear of chastisement can oblige them to perform any laborious duty: slavery is there more recognizable to reason."[22] His conclusion resorted to the standard issue of the era: "It is impossible for us to suppose that these beings should be men; because if we supposed them to be men, one would begin to believe we ourselves were not Christians."[23]

The Scottish philosopher David Hume produced "Of National Characteristics" in 1748. This served as a major source of proslavery arguments and anti-Black educational propaganda. Hume was convinced that people living near the poles and in the tropical regions were inferior to those in temperate zones. He, like many before him and after him, appealed to the Greeks as the proving ground for his assertions. Greeks lived in a temperate climate, and Greeks were the models of civilization, intellect, and morality. Therefore those who deviated from the ideal were inferior. In a footnote added in the 1753–54 edition, Hume stated:

> I am apt to suspect the negroes, and in general all other species of men (for there are four or five different kinds) to be naturally inferior to whites. There never was a civilized nation of any other complexion than white, nor even any individual eminent either in action or speculation. No ingenious manufactures amongst them, no arts, no sciences. . . .
>
> In Jamaica indeed they talk of one negro as a man of parts and learning; but 'tis likely he is admired for very slender accomplishments, like a parrot, who speaks a few words plainly.[24]

Immanuel Kant based his ideas heavily on Hume's claims. In his *Observations on the Feeling of the Beautiful and Sublime,* Kant names Hume directly:

> Mr. Hume challenges anyone to cite a simple example in which a negro has shown talents, and asserts that among the hundreds of thousands of blacks who are transported elsewhere from their countries, although many of them have even been set free, still not a single one was ever found who presented anything great in art or science or any other praiseworthy quality, even though among the whites some continually rise aloft from the lowest rabble, and through superior gifts earn respect in the world. So fundamental is this difference between the two races of man, and it appears to be as great in regard to mental capacities as in color.[25]

Later, Kant replied to advice that a Black person gave to Father Labat that "it might be that there was something in this which perhaps deserved to be considered; but in short, this fellow was quite black from head to foot, a clear proof that what he said was stupid."[26]

Even Thomas Jefferson did not escape this chorus of White supremacy masquerading as dispassionate reason. In *Notes on the State of Virginia* (1781–1782) Jefferson was clear:

Comparing them by their faculties of memory, reason, and imagination, it appears to me, that in memory they are equal to whites; in reason, much inferior . . . and that in imagination they are dull, tasteless, and anomalous. . . . Never yet could I find that a black had uttered a thought above the level of plain narration; never see even an elementary trait of painting or sculpture.[27]

The work of Frank Snowden dissuades the notion that Enlightenment recovery of classical antiquity meant the inevitable rise of White supremacy.[28] Snowden argues that racial prejudice did not exist in classical antiquity. In the first major encounter with Blacks in a predominantly White society, intellectuals entertained the idea of Black equality in beauty, culture, and intellectual capacity. Herodotus called Ethiopians the most handsome people on earth, and Philostratus spoke of the charming Ethiopians with their strange color. The poet Martial sought a "super-black" woman rather than a White one.

There was a measurable lull in writing about Blacks between 1793 and 1807. However, Delores Williams points out that the 1840 United States census (the sixth annual one) was full of distortions and lies about Blacks. Although Dr. Edward Jarvis, a White doctor living in Massachusetts, uncovered the deception and published his findings in the *American Journal of Medical Science,* his work did not receive wide hearing. This was the first census to record the number of mentally ill (classified as "insane and idiots"). The census suggested that freedom in the North led to widespread insanity and idiocy among northern Blacks. This ludicrous nature of such claims was highlighted by the fact that the census reported insane Blacks in counties where no Blacks lived. John Quincy Adams read Jarvis's findings and tried repeatedly to get the U.S. Congress to denounce the census—it never did. When Adams confronted John Calhoun about the errors in the census, Calhoun stated, "There were so many errors they balanced another and led to the same conclusion as if they were all correct."[29] Calhoun later used the 1840 census to bolster his argument to admit Texas to the Union as a slave state.

Several magazines and journals popularized these views. By the time of the Civil War, the United States public was convinced that Blacks were intellectually inferior. These subtle and blatant devaluations of the color black and the elevation of the color white were and are communicated daily. Even as Blacks organized and began to enter the paid labor market, they were thrown into competition with poor White workers. This caused bitterness and tension as White employers often had a low opinion of poor Whites (often characterized as shiftless and lazy) and preferred Black workers. Williams points out that the reasons behind this dynamic were far from progressive. The poor Whites would not work for the lower wages exslaves would, they would not take jobs they felt were "Negro jobs," and they believed their common Whiteness created a social bond between them and their White employer.[30]

During the Franklin Roosevelt administration, the tendency was to decrease work subsidies to Blacks because some White welfare administrators and fact finders had a low opinion of Black intellect. Harry Hopkins, head of the Federal Emergency Relief Administration, commissioned Lorena Hickok to prepare reports for Roosevelt to use as he dealt with the victims of the Great Depression. Hickok interviewed victims, employers, and others from 1934 to 1935. She characterized Blacks as "rather terrifying . . . in appearance. They seem so much bigger and blacker than Negroes up North, and many of them look more like apes than like men."[31] She went on to suggest that Blacks should always be poor with or without an economic depression.

WITH SOULS WALLED UP IN A DARKNESS DEEPER THAN MIDNIGHT

But what about perceptions among Black folk? Colorism—interiorized color consciousness that draws out the various shades of complexion among Black folk, hair texture, and physical features—proceeds to rip us apart as a community of the Spirit. Colorism is a complex system of color grading that ranges from virtually white to brown to black. The shade of color is often directly related to social class.

In the midst of White hegemony, miscegenation created mulattoes that were extremely problematic for the maintenance of slavocracy. In the United States, all persons with perceptible Black ancestry are grouped together socially and legally. The result is that the definition for mulatto is social rather than genetic. The term is borrowed from Spanish and entered English usage in the New World in 1666 in Virginia. After this date, laws dealing with Black slaves began to add "and mulattoes" to make clear that mixed blood did not exempt one from slave status. Every British colony put mulattoes and Negroes in their slave codes and in the statutes that governed the conduct of free Blacks. Only Virginia and

North Carolina tried to sort through the implications of miscegenation. In 1705, the Virginia Assembly defined mulatto as a "child, grandchild, or great grand child of a negro."[32] North Carolina considered Negro ancestry to be from one-eighth to one-sixteenth.

In 1622, just three years after the first Africans were brought to North America, Virginia legislators passed the earliest antimiscegenation statutes: Africans were a lower form of life than Europeans and sexual union with Whites was bestiality on one hand and twice as evil as fornication between two Whites on the other. However, this did not stop many White masters' fornication with female slaves. The children produced from such unions were problematic—did they inherit the free status of their White father or the slave status of their Black mother. In 1662 the colonists of Virginia steered away from traditional English law and voted that these children would have the status of the mother.

It is important to note that not all mulatto offspring in the early years of the emerging nation were subject to slavery. Those exempt were children born from free coloreds, children born of free colored mothers and slave fathers, children born of White females and Black slave fathers, and most children who were of mixed Negro and Indian parentage.

Free mulattoes presented a peculiar problem—though free, how did they have this status yet not challenge slavocracy? The upper South (above Virginia) instituted the one drop rule. Legislators decided that any person with even one drop of Black blood would have the same legal status as a pure African. This was entrenched by the early 1700s and spread North and was legal precedent into the early 1800s.

Below North Carolina a different mix of slave men and women, masters, and mistresses prompted a different response. Few European women lived in these sparsely populated agricultural areas. Many White plantation owners became sexually and emotionally involved with Black female slaves and attached to children from these relationships. White legislators in this part of the land were more liberal regarding the legal status of mulattoes. In the Deep South, mulattoes even attained the status of a separate Colored class.

A three-tiered social system evolved in the lower South with mulattoes and a small number of free mulattoes as the buffer between Blacks and Whites. This small number of free mulattoes before the Revolutionary War increased after it. Authors Russell, Wilson, and Hall argue that the preferential treatment of mulattoes by Whites was the groundwork for a pattern of color classism or colorism in Black America.[33] I will return to this insight later.

The antislavery writings of the 1850s reveal the occasional praise of the mulatto as a superior human type. Writing in 1855, C. G. Parsons in *Inside Slavery, Or a Tour among the Planters* saw the mulattoes as "the best specimens of manhood found in the South. The African mothers have given them a good physical system, and the Anglo-Saxon fathers a good mental constitution."[34] After Emancipation, some writers raised the extreme position of the possibility of intentional, widespread miscegenation as a way of dampening the aggressiveness of Anglo-Saxons. Moncure Daniel Conway was a southern abolitionist who emigrated to England during the Civil War. He became disgusted with what he considered the mixed motives and sophism of the North on the slave question. In 1864 Conway wrote that "each race is stronger in some direction than all others but for that strength it has suffered loss in other directions."[35] He saw European representing intellect and energy, but deficient in the "simple godliness, kindliness, and affectionateness" that the Negro possessed. For him, the "mixture of the blacks and whites is good; that the person so produced is, under ordinarily favourable circumstances, healthy, handsome, and intelligent. Under the best circumstances, I believe that such a combination would evolve a more complete character than the unmitigated Anglo-Saxon."[36]

Bishop Gilbert Haven of the Methodist Episcopal Church in Massachusetts openly declared at the end of the Civil War that the Negro was superior to the Caucasian. He saw that the southern freed showed little animosity toward their former masters and mistresses. This, Haven believed, was evidence of "where the sweetest fountains of grace are in this land." Further, the Negro had the "most of Christ. He is the nearest to God. . . . He shall season our worldliness, selfishness, and irreligion with his heavenly salt." Haven was openly enthusiastic about intermarriage with such a race and believed that the "daughters of those haughty Southerners, who have shrank from their touch as leprous, shall gratefully accept the offers of the sons of their fathers' slaves."[37] Once again, Haven and Conway were not mainstream opinions in abolitionism.

The more likely tack among the White abolitionists was a belief in limited cultural amalgamation. Although despising the institution of slavery, many White abolitionists opposed colonization and believed that the races were sexually incompatible and that the mulatto was a degenerate type. Blacks were a distinct race that would somehow add a touch of softness to the national character that they saw as having too much Anglo-Saxon toughness and insensitivity.

The Reverend Increase Niles Tarbox of West Newton, Massachusetts, typifies this ideology. His book, *The Curse; or, the Position in the World's History Occupied by the Race of Ham,* was published in 1864 by the American Tract Society. Tarbox opposed Black deportation because, "We want them, that our harsh and grasping spirit, as a race, may be tempered by the sight of their more simple-hearted and forgiving natures. We want them that our anxious and never-resting lust for gain may be shamed and softened by their more joyous and holiday." He concluded that Blacks were "a politer and more genial race [that] . . . give some lighter and more delicate touches to our civilization and our Christianity."[38]

The 1864 Final Report of the American Freedmen's Inquiry Commission, a three-man body set up by President Lincoln to recommend policy affecting newly emancipated slaves, ruled out intermarriage as undesirable on biological grounds. In a section written by Robert Dale Owen, an Indiana reformer, and later reprinted in his *The Wrong of Slavery,* voiced a comparison of Whites and Blacks that heralded potential Black contribution to American civilization:

The Anglo-Saxon race, with its great force of character, much mental activity, an unflagging spirit of enterprise, has a certain hardness, a stubborn will, only moderate geniality, a lack of habitual cheerfulness. Its intellectual powers are stronger than its social instincts. The head predominates over the heart. There is little that is emotional in its religion. . . . It is a race more calculated to call forth respect than love, better fitted to do than to enjoy. The African race is in many respects the reverse of this. Genial, lively, docile, emotional, the affections rule; the social instincts maintain the ascendent except under cruel repression, its cheerfulness and love of mirth overflow with the exuberance of childhood. It is devotional in feeling. It is a knowing rather than a thinking race. . . . As regards the virtues of humility, loving-kindness, resignation under adversity, reliance on Divine Providence, this race exhibits these, as a general rule, in a more marked manner than does the Anglo-Saxon. . . . With time, as Civilization advances, these Christian graces of meekness and long-suffering will be rated higher than the world rates them now. With time, if we but treat these people in a Christian fashion, we shall have our reward. The softening influence of their genial spirit, diffused throughout the community, will make itself felt as an element of improvement in the national character.[39]

The people who were at the heart of this debate, the mulattoes, were either assailed as unfertile, degenerate, and short-lived or as a much needed buffer between Blacks and Whites in the United States. One group in the midst of this was the free mulattoes of the South who were free before the Civil War. They amassed property, businesses, and some measured wealth. Some chose to separate themselves from Blacks to form a different class. However, after the Civil War, this class of mulattoes no longer had freedom to distinguish them from dark-skinned Blacks. Many lost the property and wealth they gained before the war because of the viciousness and all-encompassing nature of White southern backlash. This Colored elite began to segregate themselves and actively discriminated against darker-skinned Blacks based on skin color.

Mulatto social clubs like the Bon Ton Society of Washington, D.C., and the Blue Vein Society of Nashville, Tennessee, were formed during Reconstruction.[40] They called themselves the "bona fide free" before the war and formed these clubs based on color and class, in part, to help maintain the old hierarchy. Many, mulatto and dark-skinned Blacks, thought the blue veiners were a bit much. The influence and prevalence of these clubs did not weaken until after the Harlem Renaissance of the 1920s. However, the attitudes about skin color and class persist to today.[41]

By 1870, color increasingly divided the Black community. Lighter-skinned worshipers split from the African Methodist Episcopal Church to form their own denomination—Colored Methodist Episcopal (later changed to Christian Methodist Episcopal). Fair-skinned bishops were the rule in the CME Church. This was so much the case that in a 1910 editorial in a West Virginia *Advocate,* a Black weekly, noted that "there is now but one of the dark hue, all the others being mulattoes, quadroons or octoroons."[42] The issue confronting the church was whether to choose a dark-skinned Black man for bishop or to continue to follow a self-imposed color line.

From the end of Reconstruction to World War I, the mulatto was the object of considerable fascination for Whites. This is evidenced by the sizable body of scholarly and popular literature devoted to the subject. Generally, Whites moved away from the earlier miscegenation and cultural amalgamation rhetoric to that of mulattoes being more intelligent than dark-skinned Blacks, but *not* equal to Whites. Mulattoes were leaders in the Black community while simultaneously viewed as hybrids who were morally weak and physically degenerate and stirred up trouble because they demanded greater rights and privileges for themselves.

Alfred Holt Stone, a Mississippi planter, was an authority on the race problem. He, H. Paul Douglas, and Mary Helm represent the views of those who saw mulattoes as leaders.[43] For Stone, mulattoes were a separate caste—neither Black nor White. Because of this, Blacks who were free of either mulatto or White influences were "docile, tractable and unambitious." Douglas, writing in 1909, noted that the mulatto elite had emerged as a class of Blacks whose success and leadership in the Black community should be lauded. Helm noted that mulattoes were the vast majority of the Black aristocracy. Further, color class distinctions drew mulattoes apart from "full-blooded" Negroes. Using an unintentionally astute economic analysis, Helm reasoned that the reason for this is that Blacks who continued their education beyond common school were the mulattoes, quadroons, and octoroons. She saw this as a natural selection process that proved that they were "mentally fit to survive."

At the turn of the century, color-conscious Black churches emerged with the paper bag, door, or comb tests.[44] The paper bag test involved placing an arm inside a brown paper bag. If the skin on the arm was lighter than the color of the bag, the prospective member was invited to attend church services. The door test was similar, but involved a door painted a light shade of brown. The comb test was used in Virginia, Philadelphia, and New Orleans. It featured a fine-tooth comb that was hung on a rope near the front entrance. If the prospective worshiper had hair that was too nappy and snagged the comb, entry was denied. Although these tests are no longer used, the legacy of these tests persists in congregations of some Black society churches that continue to be noticeably lighter than others.

Late-nineteenth-century and early-twentieth-century Blacks most vocal about colorism in the Black community were darker-skinned Blacks who concentrated on the light-skinned upper class. They denied the intellectual superiority of light-skinned Blacks and often emphasized them as physically weak hybrids. Upper class light-skinned Blacks were blamed for the existence of the color scale between Blacks that created a perverted system of social stratification. Therefore, personal character and worth weren't important in gaining admission to the upper class of Black society—color was.

Color discrimination was prevalent in Black preparatory schools and colleges established by and for the mulatto elite. Social clubs and biased admissions policies were common in many historic Black colleges and universities established in the 1800s.[45] Russell, Wilson, and Hall report that at the most prestigious of these schools, applicants were allegedly required to pass a color test before admission. Further, the principle mission of these schools was to groom mulattoes for middle-class living and therefore a liberal arts education was essential.

Dark-skinned students turned to vocational training when they were denied a liberal arts education. Tuskegee Institute was founded by Booker T. Washington (1881) and Mary McLeod Bethune established Bethune-Cookman College in 1927 expressly for vocational education. Although Washington was a mulatto, advocates of vocational education were often darker-skinned Blacks; those advocating a liberal arts education were mulattoes. These separate educational paths at the turn of the century further divided the Black community. Evidence began to mount that industrial education did nothing more than channel dark-skinned Blacks into low-paying jobs.[46]

The overwhelming majority of the Black elite were mulattoes—light brown to virtually white. Some critics cited color alone as what prompted Black social stratification—the lighter the skin, the higher one could ascend on the social ladder. Nannie Helen Burroughs, a dark-skinned Black woman, publicly denounced color consciousness in 1904:

Many Negroes have colorphobia as badly as the white folks have Negro-phobia. . . . Some Negro men have it. Some Negro women have it. Whole families have it, and . . . some Negro churches have it. . . . The white man who crosses the line and leaves an heir is doing a favor for some black man who would marry the most debased woman, whose only stock in trade is her color, in preference to the most royal queen in ebony.[47]

Her evidence that colorism had spread among Black folk was the preference for light marriage partners and the increased use of facial bleaches and hair straighteners.

Charleston, South Carolina (a city one Black woman noted had "two segregations"), serves as a reference point for those who were critical of color gradations between Blacks. Two organizations of the city were often cited, the Brown Fellowship Society founded in 1790 and the Society of Free Dark Men. Both organizations confined their membership to light-skinned free brown men and their descendants. The mulatto elite of Charleston continued for several generations after the Civil War. This old mulatto upper class owned slaves, Sheraton and Hepplewhite furniture, portraits painted by itinerant artists, and cemetery plots for fair-skinned Blacks.[48] Few Black churches acquired the reputation for exclusiveness as St. Mark's Episcopal Church in Charleston. Founded in 1865 by fair-skinned Blacks who had been free before the war, its membership was part of the Black social elite of the city—The Brown Fellowship Society and the Friendly Moralist Society.[49] In terms of culture, wealth, color, and antebellum social status, a gulf existed between the members of St. Mark's and the newly freed slaves that caused the new free to see the church as a bastion of snobbery.

In 1903, John E. Bruce, a well-known Black journalist whose column appeared in Black newspapers for decades under the pen name Bruce Grit, chastised relentlessly Charleston Blacks for their persisting color line. However, Bruce began his jeremiad in his 1877 critique of Washington, D.C., Colored society in his column entitled "Colored Society in Washington." Bruce, who was dark and from a slave background, consistently denounced Blacks who attempted to be leaders of the race exclusively on the basis of their light skin color and White features. He blamed fair-skinned "pin-headed dudes and dudines" for introducing color into Black society and characterized their ancestors and descendants as exploitative of the Black masses (read dark-skinned) in their own drive for supremacy.[50]

From 1877 on, the colorism of the Black elite in Washington was the topic of hostile and heated commentary. W. Calvin Chase, the editor and publisher of the *Washington Bee,* was a vocal opponent of upper-class mulattoes who were eager to win White approval and skilled at moving up the social ladder. The *Bee* ran editorials and articles to this effect from 1882 to 1920. It saw colorism in schools, churches, political contests, and social relations. The *Bee's* favorite editorial topic was the discriminatory practices of the light-skinned social elite against darker-skinned Blacks.

When Richard Greener and Robert Terrell applied to the Harvard Club as alumni and honor graduates they were turned down on racial grounds. Rather than assail the Harvard Club for such racist nonsense, Chase turned the wrath of the *Bee* editorial pages on the two men. He described Greener and Terrell as examples of fair-skinned, well-educated Blacks who were trying to abandon their race for White society. Chase would broker no argument that saw their actions as challenges to White racism and segregation.

The mournful legacy of colorism is relentless. Some Black business organizations discriminated based on skin color. W. E. B. Du Bois's "Talented Tenth" (the top 10 percent of the Negro population) had twenty-one men and two women who were guides for the progress of the Black race. Du Bois, himself a mulatto, had only one person, Phillis Wheatley Peters, on the list who was not a mulatto.[51] Throughout the twentieth century, most Black community leaders have been light-skinned—Adam Clayton Powell Jr., Walter White (the president of the National Association for the Advancement of Colored People, 1931–1955), and A. Philip Randolph (newspaper editor and head of the Brotherhood of Sleeping Car Porters) to name a few. I agree with the explanation Russell, Wilson, and Hall give for this phenomenon.[52] They argue that given the ongoing valuation of white/light over black/dark in a society that is politically and economically controlled by Whites means that those who have the lightest skin and the most Caucasian-looking features are allowed the greatest freedom. The unique privileges granted to mulattoes under slavery enabled those who chose an elitist route to advance further educationally and occupationally. Even those mulattoes who were not elitist could (can) and often did (do) excel due to lighter-skinned privilege. The result, in terms of leadership, is that a larger number of light-skinned Blacks with money and education became the Black community's most vocal and active leaders.

During the 1960s, the importance of color diminished somewhat although the undertow of colorism remained. "Black is Beautiful" rhetoric and ideology caused some dark-skinned leaders to question the militancy of light-skinned ones. Dedication to the cause was judged occasionally by how large the Afro or how willing a light-skinned radical was to sleep with a dark-skinned radical. Among the less radical Blacks, the old patterns of color prejudice remained.

In the late 1980s, Ronald Hall questioned Black students from comparable social and educational backgrounds attending a predominantly Black southern university about their career plans.[53] The result continues the sad legacy of colorism. Light-skinned students aimed for more prestigious jobs. The students claimed that skin color affected their social opportunities in the Greek system—a fact disputed by some in the system and confessed by others. From the 1920s into the 1960s "color tax" parties were common in Black fraternities. The darker the date, the higher the tax paid by the brother at the door.

Hall's survey makes clear that the perception and the reality that skin color determines how wide the doors of opportunity are open for Blacks. It *is* easier for light-skinned Blacks to get ahead. Research by sociologists Veran M. Keith and Cedric Herring done in 1991 found that dark-skinned Blacks had less income and lower standing in the Black community than light-skinned Blacks. Research done by Michael Hughes and Bradley Hertel in 1990 found that light-skinned Blacks had a ratio of difference in earnings to dark-skinned Blacks that was proportional to that between Whites and Blacks—72 cents to one dollar, dark to light.[54]

Dark-skinned Blacks have the hardest time getting ahead. Now, the visual glance is helpful. A casual perusal of inner-city, predominantly Black housing projects reveal that most of the residents are dark-skinned. There are a disproportionate number of dark-skinned inmates in the prison system, and sociologist Ozzie Edwards found that dark-skinned Blacks are more likely to report being victims of race discrimination than light-skinned Blacks—more so if they are in the lower class strata.[55] We have been both victims and victimizer.

FOR A PALTRY THIRTY PIECES OF SILVER

The damage done along gender lines is tremendous. Historically, Black women have used formulas and techniques to keep us from looking "too Negroid." Where a dark-skinned man can use his intelligence, a dark-skinned woman who feels she is unattractive may think that she has nothing to offer, whatever her intelligence. In their 1968 groundbreaking work, *Black Rage,* William Grier and Price Cobb argue that every Black girl in the United States experiences some degree of shame about her appearance. There is no shortage of products designed for the Black woman.

This began during slavery when women usually kept their heads wrapped in a bandanna, but for special occasions might straighten their hair with some kind of grease as their African ancestors may have done. For house servants this meant hog lard or butter. Field hands were forced to use axle grease. When the Afro experienced its brief renaissance, it was a political statement that carried with it a renunciation of hair-straightening products Black girls were conditioned to use from childhood.

When sociologist Bertice Berry analyzed advertisements in *Ebony, Jet,* and *Essence* between 1985 and 1987, she found that over one-third of the advertisements were for hair products. Most of the models for these products were fair-skinned with long flowing hair. Mary Helen Washington points out that the subject of the distorted standards for Black women's beauty is a frequent theme in Black women's novels. Washington believes that this indicates how deeply Black women are affected by discrimination against the shade of our skin and the texture of our hair.

Black model and businesswoman Naomi Sims maintains that the use of straighteners and dyes is not an example of colorism. She points out that the women of the Swahili and Hova of Madagascar were straightening their hair with heavy oil and parting it down the center. "Beatle bangs" can be traced to the women of Chad who twisted their hair into tiny dreadlocks and cropped it straight across the forehead. Finally, African women have been coloring their hair with henna, ocher, and plant dyes and other natural substances for centuries.[56]

The history of hair care can be rooted in an afrocentric context. The use of skin lighteners cannot be so redeemed. Black women of the nineteenth century sometimes rubbed lye directly on the skin or applied harsh acidic products that were made for floor and wall cleaning. None of these things worked, nor was the mother successful who tried to lighten her daughter's skin by dunking her in a tub of bleach every day.

During the 1920s, Ro-Zol bleach, initially developed as a solution to remove skin defects and discolorations, was a popular skin-bleaching product. It was distributed by the Black-owned Overton Hygienic Manufacturing Company. In one ad, a wealthy looking Black woman who was several shades lighter than the Black man was posed admiring herself in a small mirror amid the table covered with starched white linen and fine china cups. The ad copy read:

Ro-Zol was the first preparation made expressly for bleaching. . . . Ro-Zol does not bleach by destroying the pigmentation. . . . It is received by the pigment and combines and harmonizes to produce a remarkably satisfactory, youthful, wholesome and *whitened* complexion.[57]

Another ad copy for a bleaching cream trumpeted, "Lighten your dark skin. Race men and women, protect your future by using Black & White Ointment. Be attractive. Throw off the chains that have held you back from the prosperity that rightly belongs to you."[58]

In 1990, $44 million dollars worth of skin-bleaching products were bought in the United States. Blacks seeking lighter skin can go to special salons for full or partial body bleaching. Now chemical peels and dermabrasion do what nature did not—provide some with lighter skin. Chemical peels are painful and require hospitalization because the procedure is to burn off the top layer of pigmentation to uncover the smoother, lighter layer underneath. This process can take up to a year. Dermabrasion is more painful because it involves stripping away the uppermost layer of skin with a high speed wire or a diamond-edged brush.

With all this straightening, coloring, and lightening going on, it should not be surprising that a child's awareness and appreciation of the value of the different skin colors occurs after her or his racial awareness develops after the age of three. By the time a child enters elementary school at age seven, he or she has learned to recognize *some* subtleties of racial identity. By adolescence, Black children have well-defined stereotypes about skin color.[59]

The pioneering study done by Charles H. Parrish in the 1940s explored the nature of skin color and stereotyping in Black teenagers. He found that light to medium tones were linked to intelligence and refinement. Dark-skin tones suggest toughness, meanness, and physical strength to these youths.[60] Russell, Wilson, and Hall argue that these attitudes persist today among Black youths. Light skin is seen as feminine, dark skin as masculine. Light-skinned boys and dark-skinned girls often suffer from being at odds with this cultural stereotype. Therefore, some light-skinned Black males compensate by exaggerating their masculinity by acting (and being) tough and streetwise. However, once out of adolescence, some of these males realize the advantages of their skin color—better jobs, appearing less threatening to Whites, being more popular with women—and use these as rungs on the ladder of upward mobility. In fact, it may be that some of these males have a *clearer* identity because of having to fight so hard to have *any* identity.

BREAKING LOOSE INTO A HOLY DANCE

Giant stones have done buried your spirit, your heart, your minds, shutting you off from the precious light of salvation. . . . When you find yourself buried behind a dark stone of sin just call on the Lord.[61]

Collectively, we need an insistent Aunt Cuney, a patient Lebert Joseph, the ministrations of the older women on the boat, and the healing bath of Rosalie with her gentle-strong massage. Our spiritual lives are at stake.

The noxious legacy of color and colorism in the United States leaves African American children, men, and women in a precarious place with ourselves. It leaves us vulnerable and targeted for forces that continue to define darkness and blackness as representative of lesser forms of creation.

A spirituality that encompasses all of life, which is social witness, turns to the legacy of colorism and reviews it in relentless detail. The involved interrelationship of color and miscegenation in the United States is one that the African American community of faith has not dealt with. Many in the church continue to accept dark and light imagery without question and with no critical reflection as to the kind of subconscious damage done to our self-esteem and to our ability to function as responsible members of the body of Christ.

Aunt Cuney's insistence that Avey hear the story of Ibo Landing again is instructive for us. This tale, which is well known in African American folklore, recounts how a group of Ibo slaves either flew or walked on water back to Africa once they saw what was in store for them in the Americas.[62] As the version Marshall tells goes, they started singing and marched to the ocean and then across it. The power of the tale in the novel is that Great-aunt Cuney's own grandmother saw the Ibos do this. A personal connection is made to the story. It is immaterial if this happened to Aunt Cuney. As far as she is concerned, the story of the Ibos is as believable as Jesus walking on the water. Aunt Cuney adeptly points out that some legends are privileged and others are not.

What is important for womanist spirituality is passing on legends that affirm strength and righteous agency in the miasma of oppression. Colorism defeats this at every turn if we allow the destructive character of colorism to be our watchword for how African American folk will live out our faithfulness—or not. Legends that build up a faithful people are found in the Bible as well as in the stories and folktales of the community.

Words of wisdom for times such as these build up a sense of identity that can face the challenges of systematic oppression and unfaithful witnesses.

The story of the Ibos can be placed beside the biblical account of the Exodus to deepen and enrich our spiritual lives. How is it that a people can face tremendous odds and prevail or die? How is it that a people can find ways to survive oppression or not? What does it mean to make choices about one's life that may mean death? What is the nature of grace in our lives—individually and collectively? How often and in how many places have our ancestors gone before us and found a similar set of challenges? How did they respond? Must we repeat their mistakes and commit their sins for this season or can we build from the fragments of the past and try a new way, a better way to be people of faith who are in the midst of a blight?

These kinds of questions can be asked in the context of legends and stories of faith that affirm strength. This strength is not founded on certainty, but on trust and belief. Therefore this strength does not depend on a faith community or a faithful person "getting it right" or "being right." Rather its byword is *faith*. A spirituality of life that is social witness does not revolve around a success ethic that is grounded in measurable gains and regrettable losses. Rather, it moves in the midst of degradation to proclaim the dignity of life. Such a strength measures its power in its ability to *continually* call forth hope and righteous agency.

Such a mission grounded in righteous agency is hard work. Part of agency in this context is to recognize who we have been to one another, how we are with one another, and what we can be with one another in light of God's demand on our lives. This means continually exploring the history of Black folk on these shores and our connections not only to Africa, but to the Caribbean, to Native Americans, to Islam, to other peoples of color, and to other oppressed groups. The complexity of oppression can never be underestimated. Righteous agency continually plumbs these connections to explore how we are to live our witness that is our spirituality.

A crucial aspect of Aunt Cuney's insistence on retelling the legend of the Ibo is the importance of defining who we are and the pivotal nature of controlling who names us. We proclaim our identities as African Americans in the United States *for ourselves*. Yes, we are male and female, young, middle-aged, old, conservative, neoconservative, liberal, radical, nationalist, patriotic, anarchist. Yes, we come in a variety of colors and shapes; we have diversity of sexualities; we are a variety of religions; we have a multitude of ways to express ourselves in the arts. What we cannot afford is to have no clue about who we are.

For we can be sure that someone or some industry will be more than happy to define us to suit their purposes, their gain, their profit—not ours. We must do this for ourselves as individuals and our collective selves as a people. If we can do this, we will begin to look at the structural and emotional roots of colorism in our community.

We have a responsibility for our future. We must decide if we are going to live in an uneasy, destructive, but comfortable acquiescence to the carnage of our lives or live in communal accountability. Are we going to live with some of us filling the role of colonized victims? Or are we going to realize the great gift of who we are as African Americans and begin to roll away the giant stones of sin and degradation that *we* sometimes roll in front of the caves of our souls? We become our own jailers in the household of misery and destruction.

This is where the power of tradition and traditioning can help us move into a deep spiritual witness that challenges hegemony and evil to proclaim the acceptable year. The line from the Ibos to the great grand-mothers to the great aunts to us is the line of tradition. Tradition holds us accountable to those beyond our lives, its historicity roots us in the gospel as well as in the collective story of Black folk in the Americas. We are not free to simply invent our tomorrows and improvise our todays. African American people of faith stand in the midst of the story and the stories of our lives.

The story of Jesus informs our witness. We must pay closer attention to the ways in which he was Immanuel and how we as partners with this witness must move into our own ministries of faithfulness and hope. This can and must be done regardless of the forces of sin and suffering. The story of Jesus, the community of faith that is birthed by this story, is one that realizes the cross does come before the resurrection. The tomb must be filled before the stone is rolled away. We are *not* called to self-abnegation, but we *are* called to a witness that may mean our lives.

This is tenuous when a whole community is placed and maintained in the role of victim. The provocative question for the Black community of faith is, How do we live into our witnessing at the foot of the cross and not be partner to our own self-destruction by the powers of Satan? We gain our cues from Scripture; our tutors are the children, men, and women who have gone before us; our touchstone is a deep and involved relationship with God in which we are never content to accept who we are as the final word of how we are to be in our lives.

The power of memory is the pulse of the spirituality that is informed by the legends that affirm strength and righteous agency in oppressive situations. To lose memory on an individual or collective level is to doom us to a fractured spirituality that keeps African American folk in a downward spiral of colorism, racism, sexism, heterosexism—we craft our own lynch nooses. Lebert Joseph provides Avey (and us) with a doorway into heritage as a stream of memories. There may be the grand narrative of oppression and suffering among Black folk in the United States, but it is not a monolithic narrative.

The stream of memories helps us unpack the destruction of miscegenation in the antebellum era. The rape of Black women and the rending of Black female and male relationships must be walked through and retold again and again. This cannot be an exercise in narcissistic navel-gazing, but told in light of survival. Through all that has systematically functioned to devalue and destroy the Black community, we are still here. There are lessons to be learned that are grounded in a tenacious witness and an intractable stubbornness that have kept and can keep our spirituality one that is strong enough to withstand injustice.

Lebert Joseph refuses to give up on Avey finding her heritage. He tells her the importance of the ancestors in maintaining one's heritage and of the dangers of forgetting this—vexation and trouble. This is where Black people of faith (and others) find ourselves today. We are living out of human social constructions of identity that do not value life in its fullness. Rather than turn to experience, Scripture, and tradition to help shape us, we rest almost exclusively on reason—flawed and biased—as the guide to living and witnessing in the world.

It is Lebert Joseph who is the physical presence in Avey's life that leads her to the door of her heritage. Our spirituality must function in such a way as this. A womanist spirituality embraces the fullness of life with its joys and sorrows and seeks to stand with the gospel in the midst of this. It is a spirituality that builds beyond pseudoscientific notions of color and race, miscegenation, and colorism. We need a patient spirituality that will stare down structural malaise and point the way to healing.

The healing ministrations of the older women on the boat from Grenada to Carriacou point to the need for community-building work that ministers to our souls, lifts our spirits (individually and collectively), assures our connection with one another and to God, pulls us beyond ourselves. These women, who remind Avey of the presiding mothers of Mount Olivet Baptist Church, help her expel the toxins of assimilation so that she can open her mind and soul to a connectedness with a heritage of survival—regardless.

The Black religious community needs to create large spaces of welcome, understanding, and confrontation from the pulpit to its religious programming. Folk need to hear the church say in a clear and unequivocal voice that our preoccupation with someone else's notion of beauty, the gradations of skin color among ourselves, the legacy of denoting darkness and blackness with evil and light and whiteness with salvation is literally killing us.

Black folk need to work with Black folk to help create positive images of the panorama of hues in our community that are not dominated by someone else's version of who we are. We must become one another's harvest and in doing so, we will begin to recognize the gift of life we have in one another and turn away from battering and stereotyping ourselves into victimage. One place to begin to gain these new images is in the life of a church that no longer condones business as usual, that transmits religiosized versions of domination and subordination.

This means we must challenge our worship and the images we use in worship. In all of the ways in which we worship, what are the images of color, maleness, femaleness, age, income, and sexuality that we have in the very way we worship and in the language of worship? Are we telling ourselves and others that we are less than other people and not even realizing it? Whose cultures are present in our worship? Do we simply *use* other folk's cultural styles or do we seek to understand them as we celebrate?

We have a real comfort zone in our worship lives. We only notice our complacency when it's challenged by the new, the different. Are we so comfortable in our worship that we have ceased to worship and become solemn assemblies lifting up burnt offerings and grain offerings? Are we seeking to massage our souls with fatted animals and singing noisy songs with harps out of tune?

The Black Church of a lived spirituality cannot content itself with protestations of holiness if there is nothing holy present in how we hold one another and act as partners with God in shaping a witness in the lives of those folk who have not yet experienced the transformation of death and grace. The older women on the boat to Carriacou could help Avey because they knew the signs of illness and they had a way to help her stay on the boat as she loosed a torrent of agony. These women tightened their grip and held her, they cushioned her as much as possible and spoke soothing words that comforted, reassured, and encouraged her to purge herself. When little was left, they continued to hold Avey and shore her up with their bodies.

This is a lived spirituality. This spirituality stands in the midst of stench and holds on to people for their lives. It is a spirituality that comes out of a community of faith that recognizes and *knows* its story in rich detail and with immediacy. It can provide comfort and sustenance before those who are seeking their lives, their identity, their wholeness have the words to name their needs. This is a spirituality born from the tragedy of the diaspora and the survival of the middle passage. It does not come from fractured notions of color and beauty.

Avey's discovery of her heritage and then her embrace of it does not come in isolation. Aunt Cuney, Lebert Joseph, the older women on the boat, and finally Lebert Joseph's daughter Rosalie help her gain the knowledge and the freedom of reclaiming a healthy heritage that enables her to have the necessary tools to face the dangers of assimilation and success for middle-class Black folk. Avey's story is a story of the community. Rosalie's amazingly tender and respectful bath after Avey's attack of vomit and diarrhea points to the need for a spirituality that respects the individual in community. Such a spirituality tells us that each of us has worth, each of us has the right to have that worth recognized and respected, each of us has a right to be known for who we are. It holds us accountable to and with one another.

If Black folk cannot live into a witnessing spirituality or help foster it in others, then we have consigned ourselves to worthlessness. For to continue in pathways in which we condone or ignore the violence we do to our minds, bodies, and souls is to allow colorism, racism, sexism, heterosexism, classism, ageism, nationalism, and other "isms" to dictate to us our values and our aspirations. We must make it personal and communal, our struggle for life in and of the Spirit.

It is out of this context that African Americans must begin to have open and honest conversations about how colorism and caste destroy the fabric of a community that is literally holding on for dear life in this nation. As people of faith, we cannot underestimate what colorism and caste do to the soul and spirit. For much of what spawns the ability to inflict intracommunity wounds concerning color is also that which holds racism, sexism, and heterosexism in place. It is a deep and abiding desire and then ability to dominate, to control, to dehumanize, to devalue. It is an abomination to the very fiber of existence.

African Americans must take this into the communal context. Our self-respect, our self-esteem, our sense of self—individually and collectively—are under assault. Colorism points to the fact that we must be concerned about what we do to ourselves and how we respond to the structural injustices. As people of faith, our spirituality must be rich enough to help us gain clarity as to why and how we allow colorism and caste to have such a strong impact on how we see the range of hues that make up the African American community. Such a spirituality will guide us into a witness that helps us decide how we are going to love ourselves and one another rather than rely on popular culture, even our own popular culture, to tell us who we have been, who we are, and where we are heading, and how we are to behave with one another in justice and hope.

The poetry of Avey Johnson's journey home is not that of the status quo. It is the remembered *Patois* of her youth that signaled a connection with those who have gone before and those who are yet to come. This different kind of poetry holds us accountable to the demands of living in a community of responsibility and one that fosters self-worth and self-esteem for others and for itself.

CHAPTER SIX

Living into an Apocalyptic Vision

BRINGING OURSELVES HOME

you can
always
tell
when old black
women
go to church
'cause they
smell so good
and after
they been
your
way
the heavy odor
lingers in
the air
and you
smile
'cause
one
day
you hope
you
can be
an
old
black
woman
too

Apocalyptic vision. Eschatological hope. These twin concepts move within womanist spirituality. The apocalyptic vision evolves from crisis and martyrdom. It is a theo-ethical, sociopolitical manifesto that refuses to accept or tolerate injustice. It seeks to overcome the discrepancy (and attendant craziness) between what is and what should be—the discrepancy between empirical reality and legitimate expectations.

Apocalyptic vision in womanist work and thought speaks prophecy and cautions the pyramidic towers of evil to beware. It reappropriates Miss Celie's words to Mr. for the corporate context:

> I curse you, I say. . . . I say, Until you do right by me, everything you touch will crumble. . . . Until you do right by me, I say, everything you even dream about will fail.[1]

Apocalyptic vision in a womanist mode is rooted in the movement of history for African American women and men. It is concerned with race, with gender, with class, with ableness, with sexuality, with age, with militarism, with life, with death.

A womanist spirituality is concrete, particular, universal, relevant, relentless, self-critical, communal. In short, it is social witness, but it is not monolithic. Apocalyptic vision enables womanist spirituality to move with Miss Celie, Shug, and Albert as they find their way into wholeness. It dances with Baby Suggs in the Clearing. It is made whole with Avey Johnson. Womanist spirituality holds all these individual and corporate realities in a rigorous hermeneutical circle that moves beyond the known to the unknown and pushes for a rock-steady testament of the faithful who refuse to accept a world as interpreted through the eyes of those who are the key masters and mistresses of hegemony.

A womanist spirituality is drawn to question continually the inordinate amount of suffering that is the lot of the oppressed. Spirituality is challenged to a new awareness of God's presence within humanity as a liberating event. Situations of oppression do not reveal the mystery of God's love. The revelation of God's love manifests itself in work to end oppression. Hence, Ida B. Wells's words to twelve African American men jailed unjustly in Elaine, Arkansas, are the zenith of a womanist spirituality that raises radical questions on the nature of suffering:

> I have been listening to you for nearly two hours. You have talked and sung and prayed about dying, and forgiving your enemies, and of feeling sure

you are going to be received in the New Jerusalem. . . . But why don't you pray to live and ask to be freed? . . . Let all of your songs and prayers hereafter be songs of faith and hope that God will set you free. . . . Quit talking about dying; if you believe your God is all powerful, believe he is powerful enough to open these prison doors, and say so. . . . Pray to live and believe you are going to get out.[2]

The prayer to live and to believe in justice stares down suffering with an apocalyptic vision. This is not an apocalypse of gloom and doom. It does not exhort a kind of fascination with utter destruction that simply begets a passivity of inaction, and worse indifference. It does not appeal to a wrathful God who is sending the four horsemen even as millions of us kill millions of us through starvation, war, and greed. The apocalyptic vision that demands a cold, hard womanist stare at suffering rejects its inevitability and chooses life over extinction. The passionate apocalyptic vision of a womanist ethic poses the question much as Micah posed the question: "Is it not for [us] to know justice?" (3:1).

The apocalypse is not nuclear annihilation or ecological suicide. It is, as the tradition from Isaiah to 2 Peter to Revelation suggests, a new heaven and a new earth. One in which the dominant norms are challenged and debunked. One in which a new reality and project for full humanness emerge.

However, womanist spirituality means a self-critical and reflective stance that is vital and demanding. It cannot assume the universal in considering the particular—however empirically real it may be—if there has been no critical reflection on the scope of praxis utilized. It demands a rigor in our scholarship and a commitment to our community.

The womanist ideal has a broad territory to survey. At times, the temptation may be to try to do it all. For to have a rigorous praxeological framework demands that the womanist scholar push for a critical dialogue that dares to press the limits. Hence a key challenge is to do refined analysis that is not like the proverbial first sermon preached—you say it all only to find that the church expects "mo' better" insights the next week.

A prophetic eschatology can hold womanist analytical constructs in this rigorous praxeological framework. Such eschatology envisions God accomplishing divine plans within the context of human history and also by means of human agents.[3] God acts within political events and through those in leadership to effect justice in creation. However, unlike the eschatological beliefs in the prophetic writings of the Hebrew Bible, womanist spirituality does not eschew the prophetic for the apocalyptic, but holds them in tension. Where the people of Israel lost confidence in the hope of God working in history and through human agency and turned to an apocalyptic eschatology that was pointed primarily to the future, womanist spirituality holds the eschatological and the apocalyptic in tension.

The apocalyptic vision of womanist spirituality responds to a perceived crisis in the African American community. Its task, like apocalyptic literature, is to offer an alternative picture of reality and point the community in that direction. A spirituality concerned with all of life offers comfort and hope to the faithful and models an alternative moral vision to those who live and die outside the doors of the church. Womanist spirituality stands as a protest against the demeaning and death-dealing status quo. It seeks justice in the midst of evil, peace in the midst of violence, freedom as a counterbalance to oppression, and community rather than injustice.

In a community that has as a part of its social structure an "underclass," womanist spirituality seeks to tease through the possibilities for renewal and transformation in the African American community. Such renewal and transformation is not confined to Black folk. Rather, the means for a more just society is open to all who seek to live *into* an apocalyptic vision.

Historical and spiritual perspectives are key. Such perspectives have been woven throughout this book. Yet it is the apocalyptic vision, the blaze of glory that fires the soul and witness of womanist spirituality, that helps birth and nurture movements to social witness. It is in our witness that we discover over and over again God's salvation and revelation. This is what keeps our witness alive; this is what keeps us striving to restore God's rule of hope and justice. The master narrative of equal opportunity, equal access, and equality for all in an unjust social order demands a radical witness against such cruel and death-dealing distortions of the pain and suffering too many of us must endure. A womanist spirituality must console and challenge; offer comfort and demand protest in times such as these.[4]

DISPLAYING THE MASTER NARRATIVE

The United States emerged as a world power at the end of World War II. From that period until now, the federal economic policies and corporate business strategies focused on maintaining continued economic growth, technological progress, and the avoidance of major military conflicts. As a nation, we survived the unpopular Vietnam War; the social turmoil of the 1960s; the assassinations of the Kennedys, Martin Luther King Jr., Malcolm X, and other leaders; the near impeachment of President Nixon, and the Iran hostage crisis of the late 1970s. Our economy was (and remains) tied to free enterprise and entrepreneurship. However, by 1981, the economy caused concern: inflation was at 18 percent and industry was in decline.

The election of Ronald Reagan in 1980 marked a turning point. The economy picked up with the early effects of supply-side economics and the turn away from heavy federal oversight in some areas of our lives. Reagan's policy of personal and corporate tax cuts combined with the Federal Reserve's firm control of the money supply resulted in one of the swiftest economic booms the United States has ever seen.[5] The economic growth rate reached nearly 7 percent in 1984 and inflation was less than 2 percent in 1986. There was a downside, however. The surge in domestic demands for goods sucked in imports while exports became increasingly uncompetitive because of the rise in the dollar. Lax federal fiscal policies aided the tremendous increase in the trade and budget deficits. In 1985, we became a debtor nation.

Sorting Through Myths in the Narrative

In a mixed economic picture, it becomes increasingly difficult to understand the nature and effects of poverty. Several popular myths of poverty have driven much of our economic and social policies.[6] These myths also influence our theo-ethical reflections. A helpful marker year to understand the power of these myths is 1984. This is when the benefits and the liabilities of supply-side economics became measurable and tangible.

The most vicious of the myths is that the poor refuse to work and prefer to live off welfare. In 1984, 7.3 million families lived in poverty. More than half of these families had at least one worker, and more than 20 percent had two or more workers. In the same year, an additional 1.4

million able-bodied poor sought work and were unable to find it. Only one-third of poor families received public assistance and only 43 percent received food stamps.

A second myth is that most poor folks are Black, members of households headed by women, and reside in inner-city ghettos. In 1984, more than two-thirds of the 34 million people living in poverty were White, fewer than 10 million were Black. Between 1978 and 1984, the number of Whites in poverty grew by 41 percent compared to 25 percent for Blacks. Only one-third of the poor live in female-headed families while two-thirds of poor families live in rural or suburban areas. Less than one-fifth of the poor live in inner-city ghettos. Poverty increased more rapidly among those living in married couple or male-headed households than among those in female-headed households.

A third myth is that welfare payments are the major factor underlying the growing federal deficit. Aid for Dependent Children (AFDC) cost $8 million in fiscal year 1984. This is 5 percent of what was spent on social security and less than 4 percent of the defense budget. Since 1972, the median benefits paid in welfare programs declined 33 percent in purchasing power. Programs aiding the middle class and the elderly kept pace with inflation.

A fourth myth is that workfare programs will solve the poverty problem. Unfortunately, work programs do not guarantee jobs. There must be an extensive job network and placement mechanism that helps participants in workfare programs acquire jobs that can move them and their families into long-term, and preferably life-long, independent living.

When we talk about welfare, most of us mean AFDC, and growing numbers of us believe that the "massive" expenditures on welfare have failed to make a significant structural dent on poverty. The perception that the U.S. welfare state has grown dramatically over the past two decades is accurate. However, welfare is not the same as the welfare state. The aim of the welfare state is not to alleviate poverty. Its aim is to insure workers and their families against common risks. Therefore, social welfare spending (that pertaining to the welfare state) and welfare spending (that pertaining to AFDC and other welfare programs that are antipoverty programs[7]) have not taken the same path—although welfare spending is a substantial and growing component of the U.S. welfare state, spending was lower in 1987 than in 1971. For instance, in relation to total federal spending, by 1990, AFDC had been cut in half since 1973.

Morality and Poverty

Poverty and morality have a labyrinthine correlation for those who are prosperous or endure manageable suffering in an unjust social order. Our images of class and social position are intricately (and often subconsciously) linked with moral suasion. Therefore, African Americans are in a peculiar, if not precarious, position in the United States. The disproportionate number of Black folk living below the poverty line and the historic roots of persistent poverty among African Americans remain the focus. It matters little that the true locus of poverty in the United States is not Black, northern, or urban. Data from the 1990 census reveals a different United States.[8] Poor Whites outnumber poor Blacks by a ratio of two to one. Most of those participating in Aid to Families with Dependent Children (AFDC) are not Black. Jacquelyn Jones reveals more disruptive statistics.[9] Poverty is greatest in Texas, South Dakota, and Missouri. There are more southerners living below the poverty line than people living in the Northeast and the Midwest. Indeed, the South has the highest proportion of poor children. Less than half of poor children live in inner-city areas. Concomitantly, Black female-headed households in rural areas were more numerous than those in the inner city.

However, the picture *in* Black America is troubling. The poverty rate among Blacks was 28 percent (8.8 percent among Whites) and nearly half of all African American children lived in poor households (13 percent among Whites). Of these households, nearly 75 percent were headed by a woman (14.3 percent among White families). Among poor Blacks, 60 percent lived in central cities (30 percent among Whites).

These kinds of figures mixed with a focus on Black urban ghettos prompt numerous discussions of the Black underclass. These discussions often revolve around issues of morality and behavior rather than economics and market force. Poverty in the city is viewed as dirtier than poverty in rural areas. Images of gangs, substance abuse, sexual exploitation, and violence become lodged in the Black urban core city. The Black rapist myth is revived while the systematic exploitation and dehumanization of Black women, children, and men remains *sotto voce.*

Poverty and class in the United States are endemic to the national economy *and* moral values. The contemporary state of affairs for African Americans and the nation cannot be divorced from the economic history of this country. The early exploitation of labor in the 1600s with the use of indentured servants set a pattern in the U.S. economy in which a few enjoy the profits produced by the labor of many. As modes of production and progress fired the nation's economic engines, poverty, underemployment, and unemployment produced marginalization. Those groups on the periphery were and are held there by the centrifugal force of economic growth.

This growth is *not* structured so that all can enter the labor force on equal footing. The realities of social location and history make this impossible. The most common definitions of the underclass obscure the realities of ghetto life so that *structural* and *systemic* solutions to the plight of the underclass remain illusive. As Jones notes, the working definitions tend to focus on racially segregated, hyperghettoized areas that suggest that poverty is isolated from mainstream society.[10] She points out that even the poorest urban census tracts consisted of some blue-collar workers like postal and transit workers and others whose wages were insufficient to raise them above the poverty line.

Rather than an isolated, antisocial social group, those folk who make up the underclass are a much more complex social organization that bear some care-filled consideration in the life of the African American church. For many poor households develop strategies for survival that are based on the care of children and the maintenance of family ties. They are neither immoral nor amoral, rather poor folks are struggling against an inequitable socio-economic structure that neither Emancipation nor the Civil Rights Act of 1964 or the recent election of William Jefferson Clinton as president of the United States can effectively subvert, such that large numbers of Blacks remain impoverished and marginalized politically.

Despite much of the Black neoconservative rhetoric concerning the constitutional guarantees of political equality for all U.S. citizens and the concomitant equal economic opportunities that flow from our rights, we live in a society of radical inequality where poverty effectively negates the notion of opportunity. Ghettos become the contemporary version of localized plantation economies that confine their inhabitants in an enclosed area with limited educational and employment capital.[11] For instance, although the Black high-school dropout rate fell from 27 percent to 15 percent from 1968 to 1989, these gains yielded little systemic or communal reward as entry level and low-skill job opportunities moved to the suburbs and away from municipal bus lines. Any increased Black commitment to schooling could not compensate for the loss of jobs that gave previous generations of working-class youths their start in the primary labor force.[12]

The combination of general myths about poverty and stereotypes about African Americans become deadly when the realities of Black life in the United States are added. Moral judgments against the poor, when focused on the African American community and the notion of the underclass, leave a wholly incomplete and extremely jaundiced view of the Black moral universe. Notions of the wholeness of the spirit and an apocalyptic vision become fleeting if not deemed an unattainable utopia. The womanist apocalyptic vision is grounded in the reality of the crisis in Black life and seeks to provide a means to attain the wholeness of body and spirit.

THERE IS NO COTTON TO PICK

Several factors are important for understanding the postmodern culture in which we live. Market forces have an unprecedented impact on our lives, the United States has displaced Europe as a force of global influence, and on a national scale, there is increased political polarization by race, gender, class, region, and religious viewpoint. This all takes place in a consumer-oriented society that also has at its core free enterprise and entrepreneurship. Rather than question the master narrative, as a nation we help reify and refine it. Often there are nationalist, xenophobic tones added that belie strong religious, racial, patriarchal, and homophobic overtones.[13]

The result is a drive for inclusion in the social order, rather than a radical transformation of an unjust and inequitable society. As Cornel West ably points out, inclusion does have its benefits. New perspectives and questions now have a place in communal and societal discourse. There are possibilities for new frameworks of how to be a society. However, the only ones who benefit are those who are included. Class structures are reinforced and legitimated. The underclass remains categorized as morally bankrupt and dysfunctional. There is no radical questioning or analysis of a socioeconomic order that could spawn the underclass. In the church, we remain mute and do not offer a theology or a spirituality that responds and challenges the status quo.

West argues that the influx of drugs into Black neighborhoods between 1964 and 1967 caused the disintegration of the "transclass character" of African American communities in which different classes lived together.[14] He argues that Black communities were a place that transmitted the values of self-respect and self-esteem across generational lines and through transclass interactions. However the loss of extended familial ties has created a people who are seeking positive self-identities and self-images while being assaulted with negative ones. West asserts that to live 244 years with no legal standing, social status, public worth, or economic value means that the issue of self-identity remains central.

The contrast between urban White and Black poverty becomes key to understanding the situation of the Black urban underclass. The Black urban underclass is forced to survive in conditions that define them by the physically decaying residential and commercial infrastructures, dilapidated and abandoned housing, boarded up storefronts, broken and littered sidewalks, and trash-filled vacant lots in too many locales in this country. Although the majority of poor Whites live in urban areas, only a small percentage live in the blighted poverty conditions that the Black urban underclass must endure.[15] Poor Whites tend to live in low-income suburban neighborhoods. If they are in the inner city, they tend to live in declining, but fairly well serviced, ethnic neighborhoods.

Poor Whites tend to pay less for their goods and services because the presence of a number of retailers in the neighborhood creates healthy price competition. Poor Whites also do not have the transportation costs most poor Blacks face when having to seek goods and services outside of their neighborhoods. Merchants in African American communities tend to face higher insurance costs because of their higher perceived risks and pass along the costs to Black consumers. Finally, the route out of poverty for Whites is not dead-ended and detoured by racially discriminatory barriers as it is for African Americans.

There are no significant federal programs that address the problems of the Black underclass. This is not surprising if we remember the socioeconomic structure and values we hold in a free-market economy. In many ways, the presence of poverty and the rise of the Black underclass is a logical, if not a necessary, outgrowth of our economic policies.

Rather than blame a malfunctioning economy or indict a group as morally bankrupt, perhaps a more productive and radical tack is to view the Black underclass as a hard reminder of what we have created as the norm and the social and spiritual consequence of what we understand as the status quo. In short, it is the hard face of the politics of inclusion.

The underclass is defined as the:

> Growing number of blacks who are uneducated, unskilled, unemployed and often unemployable, or employed in low-paying jobs, living in unrelieved poverty, and immersed in a culture conditioned by such abject circumstances, with only limited changes or hope for upward mobility.[16]

Mack Jones suggests that these are not new conditions for Black folk. He argues that the use of terms such as *the emerging black underclass* implies a new phenomenon that is triggered by the belief that the underclass is now permanent. It is used to imply that the members of the present underclass differ from previous generations because it is now intergenerational and self-perpetuating rather than more transient as were its antecedents.

Jones argues that this perception is misleading historically and conceptually.[17] Historically, it assumes that the underclass is a new development and does not provide any evidence to support this view. Conceptually, its narrow focus on the characteristics of the underclass obscures the interrelationship between the conditions that entrap the underclass and the normal economic forces in the United States. For Jones, it is more accurate to view the underclass as a contemporary manifestation of a long-existing phenomenon: a sizeable segment of the Black population struggling in poverty. The "new" underclass is the residual of a larger number of Black poor that existed before the rise of the Black middle and upper class that began in the 1960s.

In short, the underclass, those who live and somehow survive in poverty, is the natural consequence of a free-market economy such as ours in the United States. The *Black* underclass is now more noticeable because middle-income and upwardly mobile Black poor move out of the urban core rather than remain as in years past. The underclass is exposed where it was not before. The constantly high level of Black poverty and its 3 to 1 ratio to White poverty point to this long-standing and systemic reality of African American economic life.

The danger arises for those of us in the church who accept without analysis or critique the notion that the underclass is a new phenomenon that the Black Church must now address. The reality is that the African American church has always had before it the reality of Black folk struggling in an unequal economic arrangement. From slavery to emancipation to postmodern America, the majority of African Americans have not begun and rarely achieve equal economic footing with White folks. By concentrating on the underclass, the Black Church will lose an important opportunity to understand the full scope of its mission. Black poverty remains higher among nonmetropolitan Blacks with the poverty rate among Black people in the rural farm economy greater than the rate among Blacks living in the urban core. An apocalyptic vision of Black poverty must consider the absolute linkage between urban and rural poverty and begin to develop an integrated analysis and theo-ethical vision for how the church can respond to Black people's lives rather than Black life in the urban core.

To understand the nature of the crisis for Black people as we enter the twenty-first century is to recognize that the *routine* U.S. political economy creates conditions that give rise to the underclass. From the end of slavery until 1959, the majority of African Americans were classified as poor. There were periodic windows of opportunity that created the rise of the Black middle class. However, there has always been a large segment of Black folk who have had no realistic chance for upward mobility. As Jones suggests, in earlier eras the underclass was a smaller proportion of the poor. But as more upwardly mobile poor moved into nonpoverty positions, the underclass became visible.

A Question of Values

This turns us again to questions of morals and values. In the United States, poverty has been judged as a moral flaw by government policies and religious communities. Rather than explore the structures of our society that promote and encourage a poverty class, the church has often functioned as a state religion to preach and teach a prosperity gospel based on an aberration of the Protestant work ethic. Too often the African American religious community has lost its prophetic edge and turned from an apocalyptic vision to encourage a radical self-critique without advocating an equally radical societal critique. The values advocated are those of human success and prosperity rather than biblically based principles of justice and love.

To tackle poverty is to take on a task that means the church must move beyond the standard discourse of political ideologies. Political conservatives often focus on the character of members of the underclass while political liberals focus on the social structures. Both are correct to a point, but both fail to appreciate fully how social structures influence the way we think.[18] If our place in the structure provides relative comfort and the possibility for stability and even upward mobility, it is natural that we become advocates for the structure and live out values that hold the structure in place—lawfulness, educational achievement, careerism. However, when one's place is that of abject poverty such values are systematically nearly unattainable or completely unattainable.

Political liberals point to the need to guarantee equal opportunity for groups of the dispossessed and the need for the state to play an active role in this process. This touches off a heated debate in which the poor have little say. Political conservatives argue that equal housing and job legislation exists and there is no need to add any more. They neglect to discuss how effectively this legislation is enforced. Liberals continue to advocate the role of state, but fail to realize that enforcement of civil rights laws will not ultimately solve the problems facing the underclass. For the laws are designed to "fix" the system, not change it or challenge it structurally.

This places the Black poor in a precarious position. The myth that racism no longer exists is supported by the reality of a growing Black upper and middle class. Some Black scholars point to the values of the Black underclass as the reason for its predicament. In other words, these scholars suggest that opportunities exist for poor Blacks, but the members of the underclass fail to take advantage of these opportunities because they are "lazy, undisciplined, and too prone to satisfying their immediate desires."[19]

These are highly charged moral claims that place the sole responsibility for Black poverty and the state of the Black underclass at the door of the structural victims. Howard McGary points out that being lazy means being resistant to work or preferring idleness. He argues that it is not clear that the Black underclass is resistant to work, for to be lazy means there must be a genuine opportunity for the person to engage in meaningful and nonexploitative work. For McGary, the Black underclass is not turning down good-paying, safe, and non-dead-end jobs.[20] He questions whether it is rational for mothers heading single-family households to accept jobs that do not have health plans and child care services that they can receive through social welfare programs.

This is a question for the mainstream church that is often middle-class in either its membership or values. In advocating a bootstrap approach to economic upward mobility, does the mainstream African American church also condone a socioeconomic order that places some of its actual or potential constituency in a moral no-win situation? There are times when no job is better than any job in our free-market economy and social welfare system. The high value on work is healthy when one is able to enter the market and achieve some measure of independent living that secures the possibility of a viable existence. Those who criticize the Black underclass for its lack of values may well recognize the harshness of the conditions, but quickly answer that toughness and resourcefulness is required to survive. In addition, embracing values that have proven "successful" will improve the lot of the poor.

This is the mainstream Black Church practicing dominant ethics in its most deadly form. Religious reflection based on the belief that the system in which we live is just cannot respond to those who have little to no evidence that we live in a just society. Religious reflection grounded in the knowledge that the system we survive in is unjust, but only requires reform, will miss the mark with those who lack the material things many of us take for granted. The Black Church faces, as part of its social witness, those who know that what they are given is at best modest opportunities and resources to combat yawing odds for success. And rather than most of us facing such a reality, only certain of us—the dispossessed and the poor—face such an uphill and inequitable struggle.

The number of Black churches in declining neighborhoods, in which the members of the church who largely represent the middle class that has left these communities, continues to grow. Communities that once consisted of the affluent, the poor, the criminal, and the working class now have three major groups—those working to get out, those too poor to ever get out, and the criminal element.[21] As U.S. society opened up, those who could afford to move left behind the poor and the criminal element, and the community deteriorated. These members took with them the tax base and a large measure of the stability a tax base brings with it. These churches sit in large, urban black communities populated

133

with Blacks at the bottom or near the bottom of the economic ladder. The witness of the church is muted because the members of the church have left the community to return on Sundays and perhaps for weekday meetings that involve the physical survival of *the church,* but does not address the spiritual or physical needs of *the community.*

In growing numbers of Black urban neighborhoods, the community does not have as a major resource for the daily struggle for survival and stability the very church that sits in its midst. Rather than partnership, antagonism becomes the watchword. The church becomes a physical and highly visible reminder of the growing chasm between poor Blacks and those who are at all levels of the middle class. Middle-class Black flight means that the underclass that is left behind now loses a key historic resource to combat the consequences of structured social inequality. And in too many instances, the middle-class Black Church reflects the moral judgment of the larger socio-economic order against the poor and the dispossessed.

This leaves as the sociomoral guardians of the community the smaller storefront churches and lower class mainline churches. These churches struggle with the Black underclass in an often valiant effort to attain and maintain viable living standards. However, there is the reality and the possibility that the moral dictates of these churches provide yet another front for the maintenance of the status quo by turning the very set of moral values that helps sustain the community on its head as a straitjacket of moral dicta. These dicta function to draw yet another circle around the church that often leaves out substance abusers, single parents, the homeless, gay men and lesbians, the mentally ill, and people with handicapping conditions. In short, only certain members of the underclass and those who survive in poverty find a place to carry on moral reflection about the nature of their faith and the consequences of their spirituality.

Key to the discussion at this point is the awareness that the Black Church, regardless of the socioeconomic class location of its members, must draw a line between what people do as a matter of moral duty and supererogatory acts. The Black Church cannot lapse into or continue to advocate a spirituality and a social witness that preaches and teaches self-abnegation and moral intolerance. This does not mean that the church should be the religious arbiter of an "anything-goes" spirituality. Rather, the church must gain a clearer understanding of the nature of tolerance and intolerance and begin to question the structural moral universe in which it exists and for which it is responsible.

THE MIDDLE MAY NOT HOLD

The Black underclass does not exist in a system that has within it genuine opportunities for all peoples. The response to such a system is far from monolithic for Black folks. Some have faced the system of choices we have in the United States and have succeeded in some measure. Others have been consumed and destroyed. This challenges the church to realize that the answers to poverty and the visible Black underclass cannot be simplistic. When Black neoconservatives talk about opportunities, they typically mean that jobs are available for those who are willing to work. These jobs are usually those that either require highly specialized skills or those in service industries that require minimal skills.

This raises the question why, if these jobs are available, there is no effective way of systemic recruitment or training process by those who are offering these jobs.[22] McGary points out that one must be positioned to take advantage of opportunities. This means education, training, and a work ethic. However, we must also consider factors such as health care and environmental hazards that affect the underclass in disproportionate numbers. The existence of opportunities must mean more than the availability of jobs. Factors such as the accessibility of jobs—transportation to and affordable housing near possible jobs—are also key.

Having lifted up flight as a key fault of the Black middle-class mainstream church, it is important to examine the Black middle class to explore what possibilities there are for developing an effective social witness and vital spirituality that can respond to poverty and the visible Black underclass. For it is the middle class that is often pressured to see itself as obligated to help other Blacks *because* of its success. Will this middle hold us?

The African American middle class is not only an income group. It is a group made up of lawyers, doctors, realtors, ministers, corporate managers, venture capitalists, bankers, and business owners.[23] This Black professional and entrepreneurial class existed before Emancipation and in the intervening years had provided the bulk of the leadership found in the African American community. The defeat of Reconstruction with its massive political setbacks meant that the Black middle class grew within the context of the Jim Crow segregation. The development of this class was circumscribed by the boundaries imposed on it by White America: mortuaries, insurance companies that served Blacks, banks, and the cosmetic industry. This class was excluded from important sections of the economy and geographically confined.

Contemporary Black Neoconservatism Revisited

As William Fletcher and Eugene Newport point out, the social, political, and economic restriction of the Black middle class also influenced the overall strategies for Black economic and social development. As they assert, the class demands of the Black middle class found their way into the agenda of the Civil Rights Movement such that the class values, desires, and needs were cast as those for all Black Americans.

This produced some positive gains for the African American community. Victories in civil rights legislation and judicial decisions shattered economic and social barriers. However, when corporate America discovered the tremendous consumer base in the Black community, Black business suffered when unable to compete with the greater resources corporate business had to promote products and encourage consumerism. The end of legal segregation *and* the disruption of the Black economic community threw many of the political organizations that represented the traditional Black middle class into disarray. The National Association for the Advancement of Colored People (NAACP) did not have a swift and effective response for the traditional middle class, and they did not loyally speak for the upwardly mobile sector.[24]

Contemporary Black neoconservatism grew in this environment. Fletcher and Newport assert that one segment of neoconservatism came from those who were both beneficiaries of victories from the 1960s and those who served newly developing industries such as information processing and financial management. They point to a sector of "reactionary virulently anti-community and homophobic . . . fundamentalist black clergy"[25] as the other. This sector has responded to the ideological and political vacuum in African American life with a set of "traditional values" that draws a large circle of exclusion in which the Black Church does its ministry and witness.

Moral Dilemmas

In general, issues of self-doubt, self-contempt, self-hatred, and self-flagellation are daily fare for all African Americans. Many middle-class Blacks are morally torn between their feelings of obligation to other Blacks and their desire to take advantage of the social progress. This obligation comes from the ties of a group identity and the challenges of survival in an unjust social order. Many African Americans feel a deep commitment to the Black community broadly defined and seek its overall health and welfare. However, the cost of staying in decaying and crime-ridden communities is often seen as over and beyond what the middle class owes the Black community. These are hard choices and realities for those who come from a community that needs to retrieve its transclass character in order to survive. The Black Church can be the place that provides the proving ground for the return of some middle-class Blacks to poor communities to help stabilize and rebuild those communities that are deteriorating.

At times, appropriately, the Black middle class is being blamed for the condition of poor urban African Americans. There does seem to be a different political and economic agenda between the two groups, but there is a common base from which to build. Many inner cities have structurally sound, low-cost housing that can be used as a financial inducement. The Black community, even those who survive in poverty and may be members of the underclass, are consumers. These provide a base for Black owned and operated business. However, to model flight from the problems of the urban core is to model values that do nothing to change the basic structure of our society. This is needed if poor Blacks and the underclass are to receive help that can effect structural and systemic change.

This means addressing what Cornel West calls our culture of consumption. West points out that for the first time in our history as a people in this land, there are no longer viable institutions and structures that can effectively transmit the values of hope, virtue, sacrifice, risk, and putting the needs of others higher or in tandem with ourselves.[26] There is a breakdown in the moral fabric of Black life, but it is one that is far more insidious and death-dealing than the moral judgments lodged against the poor and the underclass by our larger social order or Black neoconservative thought. The loss of values is shaped by the larger structural realities of a free-market culture of consumption.

A key value we must regain is that of accountability. This means a respect-filled communal dialogue with a transclass base. The church can provide the arena for such an ongoing dialogue. We must begin with the reality that slavery spawned the beginning of the underclass, and there has always been a Black underclass since the end of slavery. We are dealing with a structural problem that no Black private institution or group of private institutions can solve on their own. Perhaps the only private institutions with the resources to do so are multinational corporations, and it would be foolish to expect them to take on a major problem such as poverty or the Black underclass.

West asserts that relying on the Black middle class alone as the source of the redemption of the Black underclass is a hoax. He points out that no middle class in the modern world has been cast as the source of resolution for economic and sociopolitical injustice. The reason is that the middle class does not have the resources to do this. This is certainly true for the Black middle class. Economically, Black businesses tend to remain in the lower levels of the entrepreneurial sector where the multinational corporations reign as the major controllers of the resources.

The beginning of an effective structural solution becomes the realm of politics. The Black Church can provide the arena for strategizing and organizing to effect political and social change. This means holding organization and mobilization as not only political values, but spiritual ones as well. A spirituality that tackles all of life, that understands the apocalyptic, that is grounded in the harsh realities of daily survival for many African Americans, and that seeks to explore new directions which integrate the various socioeconomic classes of the Black community. It moves with an agenda that broadens the vision of each class into one that eschews a mentality of relentless consumption for one of salvific redemption. There is a deep structural inequity that has prompted far too many African Americans to move away from a vision of communal hope and survival. The underclass, with all of its thorny problems, may well be endemic to life in the United States. But that life is structured by a social order that must be challenged and changed. The underclass represents the poorest of the poor. They are folks living in abject persistent poverty with no way out and dismal chances of survival. This is poverty beyond poverty.

APOCALYPTIC VISIONS

This grim picture of a part of African American life and the challenge it presents for the Black Church *is* only one part of the picture. Beyond the crisis, the catastrophe, a new salvation dawns in the womanist apocalyptic vision. This blaze of glory is found, in part, in the lives and commitments of children, men, and women of faith who seek to live their spirituality as social witness. In the midst of a class structure in the Black community that now pits us actively against one another, a spirituality that calls us to a relationship with God and through our humanness can teach us how to better relate to one another. Such a spirituality is grounded in the reality that our lives are both concrete and inspired by the Spirit. We are a living gospel that is shaped by our individual and corporate God-wrestling.

Spirituality as social witness means a lived experience of faith. We must explore how we relate to God, ourselves, others, and the rest of creation. This is a dynamic process in which God comes to us with a reconciling power that draws us into an intimate relationship with God's grace and hope. God is the major dramatist of our lives and seeks to move us into a deeper and more sustaining relationship with the Divine on the stage of human history. As we move into this reconciling relationship with God, we are also called to seek a reconciling relationship with one another. This will take a variety of forms and has no easy map to follow. But we must seek a fuller and more loving relationship with one another—children, men, and women—and learn to care for the rest of creation in respect-filled ways. It is, in short, to stand in solidarity with God's will for a new heaven and a new earth.

Womanist spirituality dawns from the apocalyptic visions of hope and salvation in the midst of our inhumanity. It is the lived experience of faith that is grounded in the context of struggling for faith and justice. This means that a key part of such a spirituality is to recognize the dualistic nature that so much of our lives have been tied to and question the healthiness of such a way of viewing and living life. This either/or existence can and does maim and kill the spirit, for it denies the interrelatedness of body and spirit. When we try to split ourselves in such a manner, it is only natural that we begin to see the social order as separate pieces that must be in competition with one another. We participate in a human-designed rating system, such that some of us are ranked higher (better, more moral, more religious) than others (inferior, lazy, godless).

Living out womanist spirituality means integrating faith and life. We begin by exploring the nature of our relationship with God. First, we recognize that we are made in God's image. This places us in a special relationship with God, and it also places us in a special relationship with one another. We are called to a new and renewed awareness of our humanness and our infinite possibilities.

We then move to exploring God's presence as the very fabric of our existence. God is both immanent and transcendent. God's presence is as close as our breathing and as awesome as the universe. Rather than rely on one image or one experience of God, we are now free to experience the fullness of God in life. God is not an option but a divine and sustaining reality in our lives.

Finally, we must deal with the fact that God's love for us is unconditional. God makes demands on us to live into our faith in radical ways, but God's love for us, as we seek to carry out our faith, is unconditional. We are called to live our lives out of the possibilities we have before us and not out of our well-acknowledged and believed shortcomings. God's love moves us to grow in compassion, understanding, and acceptance of one another. It helps begin the formation of a divine-human community based on love that is pointed toward justice. It is within our personal search for spiritual understanding that we are also engaged in the human struggle. We cannot allow rampant individualism to continue to control our faith lives in ways that move us farther in the direction of exclusivity.

The nature of the apocalypse leaves no part of our lives unscathed. From the reality of lynching—be it by rope, by environment, or by political ideology—to our images of gender and sexuality, to our search for identity and the ongoing negative impact of colorism, to the African American class structure and our struggles with poverty and the underclass, we are community that is under siege from forces outside us and forces within. The Black Church must reclaim and live out a spirituality that is its social witness.

Womanist spirituality scrutinizes the Black Church and all those in it with four direct challenges in the form of questions.

Can We Be People of Faith in the Midst of Diversity?

The agenda of the Black Church must be more than the color of the carpet, the battle over the bus ministry, the size of the church staff and budget, how many services (and at what time). This is demonic navelgazing. These are things that are important in the life of any church, but they are not its ministry and they are far from vital.

The Black Church must be in ministry with those who come through its doors, however irregularly, and with those who live and struggle outside its doors. The Black Church must become, where it is not, an active witness to the power of God working in life to change our is-ness. We must care for the African American community. We must respond to the fact that 25 percent of African American men will see prison. We must respond to the fact that AIDS hits our community in disproportionate numbers. We must respond to the fact that too many of our children are born in poverty and will live their entire lives there—if they are lucky enough to escape homelessness. We must respond to the fact that too many of our people cannot afford *in*adequate health care, let alone adequate health care. We must respond to the fact that we are living in a time when the whole nation can watch a man being brutally beaten and see his attackers be acquitted. We must respond to the fact that *if* we are lucky enough to hold jobs, Black women will still earn less.

There is plenty for the church to deal with in our community. But we cannot deal with the kinds of principalities and powers we face by remaining focused on our concerns as a people. We have to look for partners in the struggle. They may come in different colors. They may come with different agendas. They may come with a variety of gifts and liabilities. But we need to find partners who are committed to creating a world of justice and love and we hold on to what brings *us* to the table. But we have to come to the welcome table and figure out ways to respond to the mess.

What Are We Teaching the People?

Are we relying on an undefined phrase like *family values* to define what the church must teach? Are we content with politicians defining for us the mission of the church? Or are we involved in the work our souls must have by beginning with the questions: Who constitutes my family?

And whose family are you trying to tell me I belong to? And are these my kinfolk? What is family for us in this day and age? Are there a variety of images? Are there a multitude of ways to nurture and care for one another? And if they do produce nurture and care; if children, men, and women are growing in grace; if we are learning to live out of our accountability to one another; what makes this pathological or unnatural? How many of us were raised by adults who were not our biological parents? I doubt I am alone in having a Miss Rosie, Mr. Hemphill, Ms. Waddell, Bad Bill, Cousin Willie Mae, Mrs. Wynne, Mr. Butler, or Mrs. Carter as my parents when I was growing up.

What we have lost is our sense of community, our sense of family beyond ourselves. What we don't need, and what we cannot teach as a church, is a model of family values that is never who we were and can never respond to where we are. The church must teach out of its strength that is the historic Black community of faith. We need to remember and teach the folk wisdom so many of us grew up with in the pulpit. We need to remember and teach the sayings our grandparents and aunts and uncles and parents gifted us with (even though it may not have felt like a gift at the time). Those old sayings—stay out of corners, never sit with your back to the door, keep your legs together, you're walking on the rimbones of nothingness—have volumes to say to us today as we reinterpret them for this time and place. The Black Church must help us remember where we have been and teach that with a fierce determination.

What Are We Doing for the Spiritual Health of the People?

In all the ways that we worship together, what are the images of Blackness, maleness, femaleness, age, income, and sexuality that we have in the very way we worship and in the language of our worship? Are we telling ourselves we are less than others and not even realizing it? Whose culture is in our worship? And are we so tied to one cultural form of worship that we cannot bring the richness of our diversity into our spiritual lives? We only notice our complacency when it is challenged by the new, the different—that which is often another faithful way to be with God as God tries to get through to us. Are we so comfortable in our worship that we have ceased to worship and become solemn assemblies—lifting burnt offerings and grain offerings, seeking to massage our souls with fatted animals, singing noisy songs with harps out of tune?

What Are We Saying to the People?

One of the earliest words I can remember learning in church was *love*. I knew that Jesus loved me, that Jesus loved all the little children of the world, that love could lift me, that I should love to tell the story, and that grace was amazing.

Womanist spirituality has a nose for trouble. That is, it has a capacity to anticipate the course of events and to be prepared to recognize that angst is coming. In times like these, love without justice is asking for trouble. When what we offer folks is a restricted diet of love and do not provide an equal portion of justice, we are only talking about a partial gospel—not a whole one. Justice is that notion that each of us has worth, that each of us has the right to have that worth recognized and respected. In short, justice lets us know that we owe one another respect and the right to our dignity as children of God. If we deny justice, we are telling those who go without that they are worthless. Perhaps that is one of the reasons that the Rodney King and Malice Green beatings cut so deep into our souls. For it didn't seem to matter to some folks that no one in creation deserves to beaten like that—not in the line of duty, not because you have the power to do so. Many of us got a deep message with that verdict: Black men, Black women, Black children are worthless.

As much as we *must* preach and teach and live love, we have to do the same with justice. Love ministers to our souls, lifts our spirits, assures our connection to one another and God, pulls us beyond ourselves. Justice holds us accountable to the demands of love. It reminds us that we must always burn the midnight oil for righteousness and that you and I have a covenant and a charge to keep with one another.

It's a tall order that womanist spirituality sets forth for us. In reality, it adds its voice to any spirituality that is based on hope and refuses to accept the narrowness and death-dealing of today and only grim prospects for tomorrow. For all this, though, we cannot do it alone. For the one thing that is sure in womanist spirituality is that we must know the Spirit. Knowing the Spirit is to use both heart and head. It is to lean into God's word as both salvation and challenge. It is to allow ourselves to experience and live out of the experience of being wrapped in God's love and peace. It is to witness out of the hope we grow into with the Spirit.

It is to love God with our minds through a rigorous and relentless pursuit of grasping, however imperfectly, God's unfolding revelation in our lives through our ever-expanding understanding of the nature of the universe. It is in our struggles to live into our witness that we find God waiting for us and also prodding us into wholeness as individuals, as a people, as a church. It is in this glory that womanist spirituality finds its witness.

NOTES

INTRODUCTION

1. Alice Walker, "Womanist," in *In Search of Our Mothers' Gardens: Womanist Prose* (San Diego: Harcourt Brace Jovanovich, 1983), xixii-xixiii.
2. Walker, "In Search of Our Mothers' Gardens," in Ibid., 241-42.
3. Alice Walker, "Womanist," in Ibid., xixiii.

1. THE SPIRIT THAT MOVES US

1. C. Eric Lincoln, *Race, Religion, and the Continuing American Dilemma* (New York: Hill and Wang, 1984), 60.
2. Erskine Clarke, *Wrestlin' Jacob: A Portrait of Religion in the Old South* (Atlanta: John Knox Press, 1979), 8.
3. "How the Slaves Worshipped," *The Days When the Animals Talked: Black American Folktales and How They Came to Be*, ed. William John Faulkner (Chicago: Follett Publishing, 1977), 52-59.
4. Melville J. Herskovits, *The Myth of the Negro Past* (Boston: Beacon Press, 1958), 207.
5. Adolph B. Benson, ed., *America of the Fifties: Letters of Fredrika Bremer* (New York: The American-Scandinavian Foundation, 1924), 117.
6. Albert J. Raboteau, *Slave Religion: The "Invisible Institution" in the Antebellum South* (New York: Oxford University Press, 1978), 68-69.
7. Donald G. Mathews, *Religion in the Old South* (Chicago: University of Chicago Press, 1977), 224. Beginning in 1822 with the Stono Rebellion of Denmark Vesey to the 1831 Nat Turner revolt to the Civil War, whites tried to keep in direct contact with all black religious activities.
8. Faulkner, *The Days When the Animals Talked*, 54.
9. There are two schools of thought concerning the linkages between African spirit possession and the shouting found in revivalist American evangelicalism. Herskovits, *The Myth of the Negro Past*, 215-23 and Zora Neale Hurston, *The Sanctified Church* (Berkeley: Turtle Island Press, 1981), 91-92, argue for a close association between the

two. Raboteau, 63-64 questions this link. Raboteau suggests that it is the Holy Spirit who mounts the worshiper, not African gods. This is a valid point, however, Raboteau fails to appreciate fully the depth of blending between African and Christian cosmologies. The state of possession was familiar to slaves. Their acceptance of a Christian God replaced the myriad gods of Africa as the object who enters and renews the person.

10. Herskovits, *The Myth of the Negro Past*, 222.

11. Ibid., 233.

12. Robert Farris Thompson and Joseph Corner, *The Four Moments of the Sun: Kongo Art in Two Worlds* (Washington, D.C.: National Gallery of Art, 1981), 44. The Christian cross resembles the Kongo cross. The horizontal line, *Kalunga*, which is the name of God, is interpreted as water—either river or sea. Above the line extends heaven, and below it is found the earth. Between earth and heaven stands the mount of the living and the mount of the dead. This parallels the Christian understanding of baptism as a dying and rising to new life.

13. Paul E. Johnson, *Shopkeeper's Millennium: Society and Revivals in Rochester, New York 1815-1837* (New York: Hill and Wang, 1978), 116.

14. Rhys Isaac, *The Transformation of Virginia: 1740–1790* (Chapel Hill: University of North Carolina, 1982), 306.

15. Raboteau, *Slave Religion*, 244-45.

16. Mechal Sobel, *Trabelin' On: The Slave Journey to an Afro-Baptist Faith* (Princeton: Princeton University Press, 1988), 90.

17. Mathews, *Religion in the Old South*, 214-15. Conversion was also a release from the tension between God's expectation of perfection and human inability to achieve it.

18. Ibid., 215.

19. Raboteau, *Slave Religion*, 293.

20. Clarke, *Wrestlin' Jacob*, 40.

21. Raboteau, *Slave Religion*, 294-96; 301.

22. Henry Highland Garnet, *Walker's Appeal, With a Brief Sketch of His Life* (New York: J. H. Tobitt, 1848). Walker's *Appeal to the Coloured Citizens of the World* written in 1829 was steeped in religious imagery and prophecy. He predicted bloody retributive justice on white slaveholders as a necessary outcome unless emancipation was immediately declared. Earl Ofari, *Let Your Motto Be Resistance* (Boston: Beacon Press, 1972), 144-53. Henry Highland Garnet's "Address to the Slaves of the United States of America" written in 1843 built on Walker's *Appeal*. Garnet's address is stunning in its dissection of slavery as an evil in the sight of God and the submission to slavery as sinful. For him, it was better to die than live in submission.

23. Gayraud Wilmore, *Black Religion and Black Radicalism: An Interpretation of the Religious History of Afro-American People*, 2nd ed., rev. and enl. (Maryknoll, N.Y.: Orbis Books, 1983), 111-13.

24. Raboteau, *Slave Religion*, 314.

25. Mathews, *Religion in the Old South*, 247. West, *Prophetic Thought in Postmodern Times*, 151.

2. FINDING THE LEGACY

1. W. E. B. Du Bois, "The Damnation of Women," chap. in *Darkwater: Voices from Within the Veil* (New York: Schocken Books, 1920), 163-69.

2. Ibid., 174-79. He cites Mary Still as one of the "early mothers of the church" and refers to her "quaint" observation: "For the purpose of mutual aid, they banded themselves together in society capacity, that they might be better able to administer to each others' sufferings and to soften their own pillows. So we find the females in the early history of the church abounding in good works and in acts of true benevolence."

3. Ibid., 180.

4. Ibid., 181.

5. Ibid., 186.

6. Ibid., 185.

7. Evelyn Brooks Higginbotham, *Righteous Discontent: The Women's Movement in the Black Baptist Church, 1880-1920* (Cambridge: Harvard University Press, 1993), 128. Although Higginbotham concentrates on women of the Black Baptist church, her observations ring true for Black women across denominational lines during this period of African American religious history and experience.

8. Ibid., 122.

9. Willie Mae Coleman, "Keeping the Faith and Disturbing the Peace: Black Women from Anti-Slavery to Women's Suffrage" (Ph.D diss., University of California, Irvine, 1982), 88. Coleman notes that Black women took the *Virginia Baptist* to task for a series of articles, which claimed that women who aspired to preach or desired suffrage were in violation of God's law. These Black sisters reminded church men that women outnumbered men in most churches and were crucial for the financial health of the church and note "when there is a question as to legislation or expenditure, then the men arise in their majesty and delegate to women the task of remembering that St. Paul said 'let the women keep silence.'"

10. Bert James Loewenberg and Ruth Bogin, eds., *Black Women in Nineteenth-Century American Life: Their Words, Their Thoughts, Their Feelings* (University Park: The Pennsylvania State University Press, 1976), 135.

11. William L. Andrews, *Sisters of the Spirit: Three Black Women's Autobiographies from the Nineteenth Century* (Bloomington: Indiana University Press, 1986), 35.

12. Higginbotham, *Righteous Discontent,* 142.

13. Fanny Barrier Williams, *The Present Status and Intellectual Progress of Colored Women* (Chicago, 1893), 8.

14. Williams, "A Northern Negro's Autobiography," *The Independent* 57, no. 2902 (14 July 1904), 96.

15. Coleman, "Keeping the Faith and Disturbing the Peace," 83.

16. Ibid.

17. Ibid., 130.

18. The textile and clothing industries are examples of this. Women traditionally did the weaving and spinning to create the cloth necessary for clothes. Both these forms of production passed into the factory where men controlled both hiring and production.

19. Coleman, "Keeping the Faith and Disturbing the Peace," 130-31. It is not clear from Oldham's rhetoric that she was advocating for the ordained ministry. It is most likely she was speaking in the broadest terms possible for ministry.

20. Ibid., 135.

21. Mrs. N. F. Mossell, *The Work of the Afro-American Woman*, 2nd ed. (New York: Oxford University Press, 1988), 125. (This work was originally published by George S. Ferguson Company in 1908. Page references are to reprint edition).

22. Ibid., 115.

23. Ibid., 120.

24. Ibid.

25. Ibid., 121.

26. Ibid., 47.

27. *A History of the Club Movement Among the Colored Women of the United States of America, As Contained in the Minutes of the Conventions, Held in Boston, July 29, 30, 31, 1895, and of the National Federation of Afro-American Women, Held in Washington, D.C., July 20, 21, 22, 1896* (n.p., 1902), 34-35.

28. Coleman, "Keeping the Faith and Disturbing the Peace," 69-70.

29. Ibid., 71.

30. Ibid., 77-78.

31. *A History of the Club Movement*, 27.

32. Coleman, 78.

33. Wilson Jeremiah Moses, *The Golden Age of Black Nationalism, 1850-1925* (New York: Oxford University Press, 1978), 103.

34. Ibid., 107.

35. Ibid., 109.

36. Ibid., 113.

37. Ibid., 116. The editors of *The Christian Educator*, sponsored by the Freedmen's Aid and Southern Education Society, told the *Era* that Jacks "has never printed a disrespectful word in his paper here against colored people. It is safe to say from what is known about the man, that he would never be even courageous enough to print the whole letter in his own paper, and look his neighbors in the face the same week."

38. Ibid., 115-16.

39. Ibid.

40. *A History of the Club Movement*, 18-19.

3. TO BE CALLED BELOVED

1. Toni Morrison, *Beloved* (New York: Alfred A. Knopf, 1987), 88-89.

2. Ibid.

3. C. Vann Woodward, *The Strange Career of Jim Crow*, 3rd ed., rev. (New York: Oxford University Press, 1974), 18.

4. Leon F. Litwack, *North of Slavery: The Negro in the Free States, 1790-1860* (Chicago: University of Chicago Press, 1961), 97.

5. Woodward, *The Strange Career of Jim Crow*, 20.

6. Quoted in ibid., 24. No source given.

7. Quoted in ibid., 26. No source given.

8. Ibid., 27.

9. Ibid., 28.

10. W. E. B. Du Bois, "An Open Letter to the Southern People (1887)," in *Against Racism: Unpublished Essays, Papers, Addresses, 1887-1961*, ed. Herbert Aptheker (Amherst: University of Massachusetts Press, 1985), 4. "Let us then, recognizing our common interests . . . work for each other's interest, casting behind us unreasonable demands on the one hand, and unreasonable prejudice on the other. We are not foolish enough to demand social equality or amalgamation, knowing full well that inexorable laws of nature regulate and control such movements. What we demand is to be recognized

as men, and to be given those civil rights which pertain to our manhood." In later years, Du Bois moved from this position radically.

11. Woodward, *The Strange Career of Jim Crow*, 69. The southern conservatives believed Blacks to be inferior, but did not conclude that an inferior race should be segregated or humiliated. Conservatives practiced paternalism *vis-à-vis* free Blacks. The southern radicals were Populists. They were vigorously antilynching and sought to bring an end to the color line and grant full rights to Blacks.

12. Ibid., 70.

13. Ibid., 81.

14. Joel Williamson, *The Crucible of Race: Black-White Relations in the American South Since Emancipation* (New York: Oxford University Press, 1984), 111.

15. Ibid., 72-73.

16. Quoted in Woodward, *The Strange Career of Jim Crow*, 72. No source given.

17. Floyd W. Crawford, "Ida B. Wells: Her Anti-Lynching Crusades in Britain and Repercussions From Them in the United States, 1958" TMs (Special Collections, Joseph Regenstein Library, University of Chicago).

18. Ibid.

19. Jacquelyn Dowd Hall, *Revolt Against Chivalry: Jessie Daniel Ames and the Women's Campaign Against Lynching* (New York: Columbia University Press, 1979), 150. See also Williamson, *The Crucible of Race*, 111-19.

20. Hall, *Revolt Against Chivalry*, 153.

21. Williamson, *The Crucible of Race*, 115. Hall, *Revolt Against Chivalry*, 148-49.

22. Hall, *Revolt Against Chivalry*, 156.

23. Ibid., 140.

24. Ibid.

25. Ibid., 144.

26. George M. Frederickson, *White Supremacy: A Comparative Study in American and South African History* (New York: Oxford University Press, 1981).

27. George M. Frederickson, *White Supremacy*, 252.

28. Morrison, *Beloved*, 88.

29. Robert D. Bullard and Beverly H. Wright, "Toxic Waste and the African American Community" in *Prescriptions and Policies: The Social Well-Being of African Americans in the 1990s*, ed. Dionne J. Jones (New Brunswick, N.J.: Transaction Publishers, 1991), 67-68.

30. Urban industrial areas often suffer from elevated air and water pollution problems. Rural areas expose the inhabitants to high levels of farm pesticides. For a more detailed description of these hazards, see Robert D. Bullard, *Dumping in Dixie: Race, Class, and Environmental Quality* (Boulder, Col.: Westview Press, 1990) and the 1987 study by the United Church of Christ Commission on Racial Justice, "Toxic Wastes and Race in the United States: A National Report on the Racial and Social-Econonic Characteristics of Communities with Hazardous Waste Sites."

31. Ibid., 68.

32. Charles Lee, "Toxic Waste and Race in the United States," in *Race and the Incidence of Environmental Hazards: A Time for Discourse*, ed. Bunyan Bryant and Paul Mohai (Boulder, Col.: Westview Press, 1992), 13.

33. Ibid.

34. Lee, "Toxic Waste and Race in the United States," 14-15. In 1991, African Americans comprised 11.7 percent of the population in the United States. The six cities that top the toxic waste sites list have a markedly higher percentage of Blacks:

	# of sites	% of blacks
Memphis, TN	173	43.3
St. Louis, MO	160	27.5
Houston, TX	152	23.6
Cleveland, OH	106	23.7
Chicago, IL	103	37.2
Atlanta, GA	94	46.1

Although economics is a factor, the single best variable to explain the siting of commercial toxic-waste facilities is race. Communities with a single hazardous waste facility have twice the percentage (24 percent versus 12 percent) of racial/ethnic folk as communities without such a facility. Communities with two or more sites have more than three times (38 percent versus 12 percent) the racial/ethnic representation than communities without such sites.

35. Harvey L. White, "Hazardous Waste Incineration and Minority Communities," in *Race and the Incidence of Environmental Hazardous: A Time for Discourse*, ed. Bunyan Bryant and Paul Mohai (Boulder, Col.: Westview Press, 1992), 131-132. The White population of Baton Rouge in the selected communities was 124,400. This averages one site for every 31,100 residents. The racial/ethnic population in the selected communities was 110,000. This averages one site for ever 7,349 residents.

36. Bullard, *Dumping on Dixie*, 7.

37. Morrison, *Beloved*, 88.

38. Employment, housing, education, economic development, and political empowerment are the traditional concerns of civil rights organizations. The environmental movement has not adequately addressed problems in racial/ethnic communities.

39. Connor Bailey and Charles E. Faupel, "Environmentalism and Civil Rights in Sumter County, Alabama," in *Race and the Incidence of Environmental Hazards: A Time for Discourse*, ed. Bunyan Bryant and Paul Mohai (Boulder, Col.: Westview Press, 1992), 141-42.

40. The first national Black environmental protest was in 1982 in predominantly Black Warren County, North Carolina, when the county was selected as the burial site for 32,000 cubic yards of soil contaminated with highly toxic PCBs (polychlorinated biphenyls). The PCBs were dumped illegally along the roadways in fourteen North Carolina counties in 1978. Although the African American-led protests were unsuccessful in halting the construction of the landfill, the protest action peopled by Black civil rights leaders, politicians, and community residents prompted Congressman Walter E. Fauntroy (Democrat, District of Columbia) to initiate the landmark 1983 GAO study of toxic waste landfill sites in the South.

41. For a thorough synopsis of Black life in the United States, see William P. O'Hare, Kelvin M. Pollard, Taynia L. Mann, and Mary M. Kent. "African Americans in the 1990s," *Population Bulletin* 46, no. 1 (Washington, D.C.: Population Reference Bureau).

42. U. S. Bureau of the Census, *Statistical Abstract of the United States: 1992*, 112th ed. (Washington, D.C., 1992), table 696. Figures for 1980 in current dollars were: $18,684 for Whites, $10,764 for Blacks, $13,651 for Hispanics. In 1990, these figures where $31,231 for Whites, $18,676 for Blacks, and $22,330 for Hispanics. When adjusted for constant 1990 dollars, the 1980 figures are $29,636 for Whites, $17,073 for

Blacks, and $21,653 for Hispanics. The increase in median family income is far from dramatic and signals that as a society, we are barely keeping pace with the cost of living.

43. Ibid., tables 696, 724, 725. The statistics reveal a complex picture. Blacks, Whites, and Hispanics all made gains in median family income from 1980 to 1990. Yet as this occurred, more folk slipped below the poverty line. The 1980 figures reveal overall, 10.3 percent of the population fell below the poverty line. This broke down to 8 percent for Whites, 28.9 percent for Blacks, and 23.2 percent for Hispanics. In 1990, 10.7 percent of the overall population was below the poverty line. This was 8.1 percent for Whites, 29.3 percent for Blacks, and 25.0 percent for Hispanics. Poor Black families are slipping deeper into poverty. From 1979 to 1989, the income deficit grew 23 percent for Black families. Families in poverty became poorer while families at the top end of the income scale grew richer. See O'Hare, et al., "African Americans in the 1990s," 31-32. One sad irony in these figures is that the official government poverty index may not capture all of the poor. When asked what income level should determine poverty, the interviewees cited a significantly higher figure.

44. O'Hare, et al., "African Americans in the 1990s," 31.

45. William Julius Wilson, *The Declining Significance of Race* (Chicago: University of Chicago Press, 1978). For a discussion of Wilson's work, see Manning Marable, *Race, Reform, and Rebellion: The Second Reconstruction in Black America, 1945-1990*, rev. ed. (Jackson: University Press of Mississippi, 1991), 157-58 and Gertrude Ezorsky, *Racism and Justice: The Case for Affirmative Action* (Ithaca, N.Y.: Cornell University Press, 1991), 65-72. Among the comments of the detractors were sociologists Harry Edwards who called it a "mediocre work with a highly controversial title." Sociologists Charles Payne and Charles Willie termed it "economic determinist of the narrower sort" and representative of "particularism" respectively.

46. Wilson, *The Truly Disadvantaged* (Chicago: University of Chicago Press, 1987).

47. Marable, *Race, Reform and Rebellion*, 201. Walter Williams of George Mason University aggressively condemned racial quotas and advocated the creation of a subminimum wage to promote Black employment. Robert Woodson, president of the National Center for Neighborhood Enterprise, advocated economic power that would then lead to sociopolitical clout.

48. Thomas Sowell, *Civil Rights: Rhetoric or Reality?* (New York: Quill, William Morrow, 1984), see esp. 77 and 130-31.

49. Ezorsky, *Racism and Justice*, 59.

50. Morrison, *Beloved*, 87.

51. Wilson, *The Truly Disadvantaged*.

52. See Katie Geneva Cannon's creative and unctuous discussion of dominant ethics in *Black Womanist Ethics* (Atlanta: Scholars Press, 1988), 2-4.

53. For an illuminating discussion of relationality as it relates to women transracially, see Marcia Y. Riggs' essay "The Logic of Interstructured Oppression: A Black Womanist Perspective" in *Redefining Sexual Ethics: A Sourcebook of Essays, Stories and Poems*, ed. Susan E. Davies and Eleanor H. Haney (Cleveland: The Pilgrim Press, 1991), esp. 99-100.

4. WRITING THE RIGHT

1. Alice Walker, *The Color Purple* (New York: Harcourt Brace Jovanovich, 1982), 166-67.

2. Delores S. Williams, "*The Color Purple*: What Was Missed," *Christianity and Crisis*, 46, No. 10, 14 July 1986.

3. Annelies Knoppers, "A Critical Theory of Gender Relations" in Mary Stewart Van Leeuwen, Project Ed., with Annelies Knoppers, Margaret L. Koch, Douglas J. Schuurman, and Helen M. Sterk, *After Eden: Facing the Challenge of Gender Reconciliation* (Grand Rapids, Mich.: Wm. B. Eerdmans Publishing Co., 1993), 226-66 (esp. 242-44). I use Knoppers broad categories with my own expansion.

4. Ibid., 249-56.

5. Christopher Daly, "Woman Charged in Death of Own Fetus in Accident," *Washington Post*, 25 November 1989, A4.

6. "Missouri Fetus Unlawfully Jailed, Suit Says," *New York Times*, 11 August 1989, B5.

7. Patricia J. Williams, *The Alchemy of Race and Rights* (Cambridge: Harvard University Press, 1991), 183-85.

8. Shahrazad Ali, *The Blackman's Guide to Understanding the Blackwoman* (Philadelphia: Civilized Publications, 1989), 11, 40, 75.

9. Herodotus, *The Histories,* trans. Aubrey de Sélincort (Baltimore: Penguin Books, 1971), 306.

10. Jean Devisse, *The Image of the Black in Western Art, Vol. II: From the Early Christian Era to the "Age of Discovery,"* Part 1: *From the Demonic Threat to the Incarnation of Sainthood* (New York: William Morrow, 1979), 39-80.

11. Sander L. Gilman, "Black Bodies, White Bodies: Toward an Iconography of Female Sexuality in Late Nineteenth Century Art, Medicine, and Literature," *Critical Inquiry* 12 (Autumn 1985), 204-42.

12. Ronald Sullivan, "Mother Accuses Sperm Bank of Mixup," *New York Times*, 9 March 1990, B1.

13. bell hooks, *Black Looks: Race and Representation* (Boston: South End Press, 1992), 96.

14. Cornel West, *Race Matters* (Boston: Beacon Press, 1993). See his provocative chapter "Black Sexuality: The Taboo Subject." Here West argues for a demythologization of Black sexuality as a way to eradicate Black self-contempt and self-hatred. West also understands the demythologization process as a means to confront and destroy a White supremacist ideology based on the degradation of Black bodies as a means to control them.

15. Michael Eric Dyson, *Reflecting Black: African-American Cultural Criticism* (Minneapolis: University of Minnesota Press, 1993), 168.

16. Ibid.

17. Ibid., 176-77.

18. Ibid., 169.

19. Robert E. Penn, "HIV and the Real Deal," *Essence* (December 1993), 46.

20. National Commission on AIDS, *The Challenge of HIV/AIDS in Communities of Color* (Washington, D.C.: The Government Printing Office, 1992), 4.

21. Alan Bavley, "Who Will Care for the Children Left by AIDS?" *Kansas City Star* 23 (January 1994), A-1, A-13.

22. "Aids Increase Most Rapidly Among Heterosexuals, CDC Says," *Philadelphia Enquirer* (11 March 1994), A-18.

23. Maya Angelou, "On the Pulse of Morning." Inaugural poem for President William Jefferson Clinton, 20 January 1993.

5. ANOTHER KIND OF POETRY

1. Joyce Pettis, "The Ancestor in Paule Marshall's *Praisesong for the Widow*," Conference on Black Writers and Their Sources, North Carolina Central University, Durham, North Carolina, 25 September 1985. Also quoted in Gay Wilentz, *Binding Cultures: Black Women Writers in Africa and the Diaspora* (Bloomington: Indiana University Press, 1992), 105.

2. Paule Marshall, *Praisesong for the Widow* (New York: Plume, 1983), 52.

3. Ibid., 25.

4. Wilentz, *Binding Cultures,* 106.

5. Marshall, *Praisesong for the Widow,* 198-203.

6. From the *Oxford English Dictionary* before the sixteenth century.

7. Winthrop D. Jordan, *White Over Black: American Attitudes Toward the Negro, 1550–1812* (Baltimore: Penguin Books, 1968), 11-12.

8. Delores S. Williams, *Sisters in the Wilderness: The Challenge of Womanist God-talk* (Maryknoll: Orbis Books, 1993), 88.

9. Ibid.

10. Jordan, *White Over Black,* 94.

11. Ibid., 95.

12. Ibid., 94.

13. Ibid.

14. See as an example William Shakespeare, *The Merchant of Venice*, II, i, 1-3. The Prince of Morocco apologized, "Mislike me not for my complexion, / The shadow'd liberty of the burnish'd sun, / To whom I am a neighbour and near bred."

15. Jordan, *White Over Black,* 16.

16. In the Genesis passage of the Noah and Ham story, Blackness is never mentioned. However the colonists interpreted the story so that Blackness and slavery were equated. Jonathan Edwards, Thomas Hooker, and George Whitefield were among the many preachers who associated the devil's habits with the color black.

17. Quoted in Jordan, *White Over Black,* 17.

18. John D. Mitchell, "An Essay upon the Causes of the Different Colours of People in Different Climates," *Philosophical Transactions of The Royal Society,* 43 (1744–45), 102-50. Also quoted in Jordan, 246-47.

19. Cornel West, *Prophesy Deliverance!: An Afro-American Revolutionary Christianity* (Philadelphia: The Westminster Press, 1982), 57.

20. See Williams' discussion of Morton, *Women of Deliverance,* 95-96.

21. Quoted in West, *Prophesy Deliverance!* 59. See also George L. Mosse, *Toward the Final Solution: A History of European Racism* (New York: Howard Fertig, 1978), 25.

22. Thomas Nugent, trans., *The Spirit of the Laws by Baron de Montesquieu,* vol. 1 (New York: Hafner Publishing Co., 1949), 240. See also Jordan, *White Over Black,* 261.

23. Quoted in West, *Prophesy Deliverance!* 61.

24. David Hume, *Essays: Moral, Political, and Literary,* vol. 1, eds. T. H. Green and T. H. Grose (London, 1875), 252.

25. Quoted in West, *Prophesy Deliverance!* 62.

26. Richard H. Popkin, "Hume's Racism," *The Philosophical Forum* 9, nos. 2-3, 218.

27. Quoted in West, *Prophesy Deliverance!* 62.

28. Frank Snowden, *Blacks in Antiquity: Ethiopians in the Greco-Roman Experience* (New York: Belknap Press, 1970). See especially pages 177-80.

29. Charles Francis Adams, ed., *Memoirs of John Quincy Adams, Comprising Portions of His Diary From 1795-1848*, vol. 12 (Philadelphia: J.B. Lippincott & Co., 1874-77), 61-62. Also quoted in Williams, *Sisters in Deliverance*, 95. See also William Stanton, *The Leopard's Spots: Scientific Attitudes Toward Race in America 1815-1859* (Chicago: University of Chicago Press, 1960). This is a study of the ways the federal government has used dishonest strategies to perpetuate the notion that Black folk are the intellectual midgets to whites.

30. Williams, *Sisters in Deliverance*, 96-97.

31. Richard Lowitt and Maurine Beasley, eds., *One Third a Nation: Lorena Hickok Report on the Great Depression* (Urbana: University of Illinois Press, 1981), 148-52.

32. Jordan, *White Over Black*, 168.

33. Kathy Russell, Midge Wilson, Ph.D., and Ronald Hall, Ph.D., *The Color Complex: The Politics of Skin Color Among African Americans* (New York: Harcourt Brace Jovanovich, Publishers, 1992), 23.

34. C. G. Parsons, M.D., *Inside Slavery, or a Tour among the Planters* (Boston, 1855), 65-66. Also quoted in George Fredrickson, *The Black Image in the White Mind: The Debate on Afro-American Character and Destiny, 1817-1914* (New York: Harper & Row, Publishers, 1971), 121.

35. Quoted in Frederickson, *The Black Image in the White Mind*, 121.

36. Moncure Daniel Conway, *Testimonies Concerning Slavery* (London, 1864), 73-77.

37. Gilbert Haven, *National Sermons* (Boston, 1869), 548-49. Also quoted in Fredrickson, *The Black Image in the White Mind*, 122.

38. Increase Niles Tarbox, *The Curse; or, The Position in the World's History Occupied by the Race of Ham* (Boston, 1864). Also quoted in Frederickson, *The Black Image in the White Mind*, 123.

39. "Final Report of the American Freedmen's Inquiry Commission to the Secretary of War, May 15, 1864," *The War of the Rebellion: Official Records of the Union and Confederate Armies, Series III, Vol. IV* (Washington, 1900), 378-79. Also quoted in Frederickson, *The Black Image in the White Mind*, 124.

40. Sadly, The Blue Vein Society is all too self-explanatory. An applicant had to be fair enough for the network of veins at the wrist to be visible to a panel of expert judges.

41. Virtually every major United States urban center has a section where predominantly light-skinned Blacks reside. In Philadelphia these are known as "lighty bright" and "banana blocks." In Chicago it is the Chatham and East Hyde Park areas and New York has sections of Harlem.

42. Charleston, West Virginia *Advocate*, quoted in Denver *Colorado Statesman*, 5 March 1910. Also quoted in Willard B. Gatewood, *Aristocrats of Color: The Black Elite, 1880-1920* (Bloomington: Indiana University Press, 1990), 27.

43. Gatewood, *Aristocrats of Color*, 150-51.

44. For a more detailed discussion of these tests see John Langston Gwaltney, *Drylongso* (New York: Random House, 1980), 80; Margo Okazawa-Rey, Tracy Robinson, and Janie V. Ward, "Black Women and the Politics of Skin Color and Hair," *Women's Study Quarterly* 14, nos. 1, 2 (1986), 13-14; Charles Parrish, "The Significance of Color in the Negro Community," Ph.D. diss., University of Chicago, 1944; and Virginia R. Dominquez, *White by Definition: Social Classification in Creole Louisiana* (New Brunswick, N.J.: Rutgers University Press, 1986), 164.

45. Russell, et al., *The Color Complex*, 28. These schools included Wilberforce (1856), Howard (1867), Fisk (1866), Atlanta University (1865), Morgan—now Morgan State

(1867), Hampton Institute—now Hampton University (1868), Spelman Women's College (1881).

46. Ibid., 29.

47. Nannie Helen Burroughs, "Not Color But Character," *Voice of the Negro* I (July 1904), 277-79. Burroughs (1883–1961) was an active Black Baptist laywoman. The Women's Auxiliary of the National Baptist Convention and the Progressive National Baptist Convention are inheritors of her legacy. Burroughs, an educator, founded the Women's Day in Baptist churches that then spread to other denominations.

48. Gatewood, *Aristocrats of Color,* 156.

49. Ibid., 281-82.

50. Ibid.

51. Du Bois' Talented Tenth were:
Ira Aldridge, actor
Benjamin Banneker, invented clock
B. K. Bruce, politician
Paul Cuffe, activist
Frederick Douglass, antislavery activist
James Durham, practiced medicine
R. B. Elliot, politician
Henry Highland Garnet, preacher
R. T. Greener, politician
Lemuel Haynes, preacher
John Langston, politician
D. A. Payne, bishop in the AME Church
J. W. C. Pennington, underground railroad
Phillis Wheatley Peters, writer
Robert Purvis, underground railroad
J. B. Russworm, governor of Liberia
McCune Smith, physician/druggist
Sojourner Truth, underground railroad
David Walker, agitator
Booker T. Washington, principal at Tuskegee
Bert Williams, comedian

In his article, "Understanding the Legacy of W. E. B. Du Bois," David G. Du Bois, a stepson, notes the elitist nature of the Talented Tenth. He points to Du Bois's own circumspection about the notion in his 1952 book *In Battle for Peace*. In 1950, Du Bois was under federal indictment as an "unregistered agent of a foreign power" in what appeared to be a move to silence and imprison him. Du Bois wrote of this episode:

> While most of my educated and well-to-do Negro friends—although by no means all—were scared by the [anti-Soviet] war propaganda and went quickly to cover, an increasing mass of Negro working class, especially the members of the so-called left wing unions, rallied to my side with faith and money. . . . My faith hitherto had been in what I once denominated the talented tenth. I now realize the ability within a people does not automatically work for its highest salvation. . . . Naturally, out of the mass of the working classes, who know life in its bitter struggle, will continually rise the real, unselfish and clear-sighted leadership.

While not a direct recognition of colorism, Du Bois has a clear understanding of the class implications. I suggest that color and class are inseparable when considering colorism. This article appears in the October, 1993 edition of *Emerge*, 62-66. See especially page 65.

52. Russell, et al., *The Color Complex,* 33-34.

53. Ibid., 30.

54. Ibid., 37-38.

55. Ibid., 38.

56. Ibid., 47-48.

57. Ibid., 50.

58. Ibid., 51.

59. Ibid., 65-66.

60. Ibid., 66.

61. Marshall, *Praisesong for the Widow,* 200-1.

62. In the actual account of the story, the Ibos, numbering somewhere near one hundred people, walked into the sea and allowed the weight of the chains to drown them. Some of the sailors who witnessed this spectacle of disaster went mad. Some were haunted by nightmares for the rest of their lives.

6. LIVING INTO AN APOCALYPTIC VISION

1. Alice Walker, *The Color Purple* (New York: Harcourt Brace Jovanovich, 1982), 175-76.

2. Ida B. Wells, *Crusade for Justice*, ed. Alfreda Duster (Chicago: University of Chicago Press, 1979), 403.

3. Mitchell G. Reddish, ed., *Apocalyptic Literature: A Reader* (Nashville: Abingdon Press, 1990), 20.

4. Ibid., 27. Although Reddish refers to apocalyptic literature, I find his description fitting for the demands of a womanist spirituality as social witness.

5. *The Economist World Atlas and Almanac* (New York: Prentice Hall Press, 1989), 122.

6. James W. Vander Zanden, *The Social Experience: An Introduction to Sociology* (New York: Random House, 1988), 240.

7. Other welfare programs include Medicaid, the Food Stamp Program, federal grant-in-aid programs such as the Supplementary Security Income Program (SSI), General Assistance, Pensions for Needy Veterans, the Earned Income Tax Credit, School Lunch Program, Special Supplemental Food Program for Women, Infants, and Children (WIC), Section 8 Housing Assistance, Low-Rent Public Housing, Pell Grants, Stafford Loans, and Head Start.

8. U.S. Department of Commerce, Bureau of the Census, "Money Income and Poverty Status in the United States, 1989," *Current Populations Reports, Consumer Income,* Series P-60, no. 169, 1990, 65-69, 109.

9. Jacquelyn Jones, *The Dispossessed: America's Underclasses from the Civil War to the Present* (New York: Basic Books, 1992), 269-70.

10. Ibid., 275.

11. Ibid., 278.

12. Ibid., 279.

13. Cornel West, *Beyond Eurocentrism and Multiculturalism, Vol. 2, Prophetic Reflections: Notes on Race and Power in America* (Monroe, Maine: Common Courage Press, 1993), 41.

14. West, *Beyond Eurocentrism and Multiculuturalism, Vol. 1, Prophetic Thought in Postmodern Times* (Monroe, Maine: Common Courage Press, 1993), 149.

15. Jeremiah Cotton, "Towards a Theory and Strategy for Black Economic Development," in *Race, Politics, and Economic Development: Community Perspectives*, ed. James Jennings (New York: Verso Press, 1992), 14.

16. Mack Jones, "The Black Underclass as Systemic Phenomenon," in Jennings, ed., *Race, Politics, and Economic Development,* 54.

17. Ibid., 54-56.

18. Howard McGary, "The Black Underclass and the Question of Values," in *The Underclass Question*, Bill E. Lawson, ed. (Philadelphia: Temple University Press, 1992), 58.

19. Ibid., 62.

20. Ibid.

21. Bill E. Lawson, "Uplifting the Race: Middle Class Blacks and the Truly Disadvantaged," in Lawson, *The Underclass Question,* 98.

22. Ibid., 67.

23. William Fletcher and Eugene Newport, "Race and Economic Development: The Need for a Black Agenda," in Jennings, *Race, Politics, and Economic Development,* 119.

24. Ibid., 120.

25. Ibid., 121.

26. West, *Prophetic Thought in Postmodern Times,* 151.

SELECTED BIBLIOGRAPHY

Bryant, Bunyan and Paul Mohai, eds. *Race and the Incidence of Environmental Hazards: A Time for Discourse*. Boulder: Westview Press, Inc., 1992.

Bullard, Robert D. *Dumping on Dixie: Race, Class, and Environmental Quality*. Boulder: Westview Press, Inc., 1990.

Cannon, Katie Geneva. *Black Womanist Ethics*. Atlanta: Scholars Press, 1988.

Clarke, Erskine. *Wrestlin' Jacob: A Portrait of Religion in the Old South*. Atlanta: John Knox Press, 1979.

Coleman, Willie Mae. "Keeping the Faith and Disturbing the Peace Black Women: From Anti-Slavery to Women's Suffrage." Ph.D. diss., University of California, Irvine, 1982.

Devisse, Jean. *The Image of the Black in Western Art, Vol. II: From the Early Christian Era to the "Age of Discovery."* New York: William Morrow, 1979.

Du Bois, W. E. B. *Darkwater: Voices from Within the Veil*. New York: Schocken Books, 1920.

Dyson, Michael Eric. *Reflecting Black: African-American Cultural Criticism*. Minneapolis: University of Minnesota Press, 1993.

Ezorsky, Gertrude. *Racism and Justice: The Case for Affirmative Action*. Ithaca: Cornell University Press, 1991.

Faulkner, William John, ed. *The Days When the Animals Talked: Black American Folktales and How They Came to Be*. Chicago: Follett Publishing, 1977.

Frederickson, George M. *The Black Image in the White Mind: The Debate on Afro-American Character and Destiny, 1817-1914*. New York: Harper & Row, 1971.

————.*White Supremacy: A Comparative Study in American and South African History*. New York: Oxford University Press, 1981.

Gilman, Sander L. "Black Bodies, White Bodies: Toward an Iconography of Female Sexuality in Late Nineteenth Century Art, Medicine, and Literature." *Critical Inquiry* 12 (Autumn 1985): 204-42.

Gwaltney, John Langston. *Drylongso*. New York: Random House, 1980.

SELECTED BIBLIOGRAPHY

Herskovits, Melville J. *The Myth of the Negro Past*. Boston: Beacon Press, 1958.

Higginbotham, Evelyn Brooks. *Righteous Discontent: The Women's Movement in the Black Baptist Church, 1880–1920*. Cambridge: Harvard University Press, 1993.

hooks, bell. *Black Looks: Race and Representation*. Boston: South End Press, 1992.

Hurston, Zora Neale. *The Sanctified Church*. Berkeley: Turtle Island Press, 1981.

Jennings, James, ed. *Race, Politics, and Economic Development: Community Perspectives*. New York: Verso, 1992.

Jones, Dionne J., ed. *Prescriptions and Policies: The Social Well-Being of African Americans in the 1990s*. New Brunswick, N.J.: Transaction Publishers, 1991.

Jones, Jacquelyn. *The Dispossessed: America's Underclasses from the Civil War to the Present*. New York: Basic Books, 1992.

Jordan, Winthrop D. *White Over Black: American Attitudes Toward the Negro, 1550–1812*. Baltimore: Penguin Books, 1968.

Knoppers, Annelies, Margaret L. Koch, Douglas J. Schuurman, and Helen M. Sterk. *After Eden: Facing the Challenge of Gender Reconciliation*. Grand Rapids: Wm. B. Eerdmans, 1993.

Lawson, Bill E., ed. *The Underclass Question*. Philadelphia: Temple University Press, 1992.

Marable, Manning. *Race, Reform, and Rebellion: The Second Reconstruction in Black America, 1945–1990*. Rev. edn., Jackson: University of Mississippi Press, 1991.

Marshall, Paule. *Praisesong for the Widow*. New York: Plume, 1983.

Mathews, Donald G. *Religion in the Old South*. Chicago: University of Chicago Press, 1977.

Morrison, Toni. *Beloved*. New York: Alfred A. Knopf, 1987.

Mossell, Mrs. N. F. *The Work of the Afro-American Woman*. 2nd ed. Philadelphia: Geo. S. Ferguson, Company, 1908. Reprint, New York: Oxford University Press, 1988.

O'Hare, William P., Kelvin M. Pollard, Taynia L. Mann, and Mary M. Kent. "African Americans in the 1990s." *Population Bulletin* 46 (July 1991).

Raboteau, Albert J. *Slave Religion: The "Invisible Institution" in the Antebellum South*. New York: Oxford University Press, 1978.

Riggs, Marcia Y. "The Logic of Interstructured Oppression: A Black Womanist Perspective." In *Redefining Sexual Ethics: A Sourcebook of Essays, Stories and Poems*, eds. Susan E. Davies and Eleanor H. Haney, 97-102. Cleveland: The Pilgrim Press, 1991.

Russell, Kathy, Midge Wilson, Ph.D., and Ronald Hall, Ph.D. *The Color Complex: The Politics of Skin Color Among African Americans*. New York: Harcourt Brace Jovanovich, 1992.

Sobel, Mechal. *Trabelin' On: The Slave Journey to an Afro-Baptist Faith*. Princeton: Princeton University Press, 1988.

U.S. Bureau of the Census. "Money Income and Poverty Status in the United States, 1989" *Current Population Reports, Consumer Income*. Series P-60, no. 169, 1990.

———. *Statistical Abstract of the United States: 1992*. 112th ed.

Walker, Alice. *The Color Purple*. New York: Harcourt Brace Jovanovich, 1982.

Walker, Alice. *In Search of Our Mother's Gardens: Womanist Prose*. New York: Harcourt Brace Jovanovich, 1983.

West, Cornel. *Beyond Eurocentrism and Multiculturalism, Vol. 1, Prophetic Thought in Postmodern Times*. Monroe, Maine: Common Courage Press, 1993.

———. *Beyond Eurocentrism and Multiculturalism, Vol. 2, Prophetic Reflections: Notes on Race and Power in America*. Monroe, Maine: Common Courage Press, 1993.

———. *Prophesy Deliverance!: An Afro-American Revolutionary Christianity*. Philadelphia: The Westminster Press, 1982.

———. *Race Matters*. Boston: Beacon Press, 1993.

Wilentz, Gay. *Binding Cultures: Black Women Writers in Africa and the Diaspora*. Bloomington: Indiana University Press, 1992.

Williams, Delores S. *Sisters in the Wilderness: The Challenge of Womanist God-talk*. Maryknoll: Orbis Books, 1993.

Williams, Patricia J. *The Alchemy of Race and Rights*. Cambridge: Harvard University Press, 1991.

Williamson, Joel. *The Crucible of Race: Black-White Relations in the American South Since Emancipation*. New York: Oxford University Press, 1984.

Wilson, William Julius. *The Declining Significance of Race*. Chicago: University of Chicago Press, 1978.

———. *The Truly Disadvantaged*. Chicago: University of Chicago Press, 1987.

Woodward, C. Vann. *The Strange Career of Jim Crow*. 3rd ed. rev. New York: Oxford University Press, 1974.